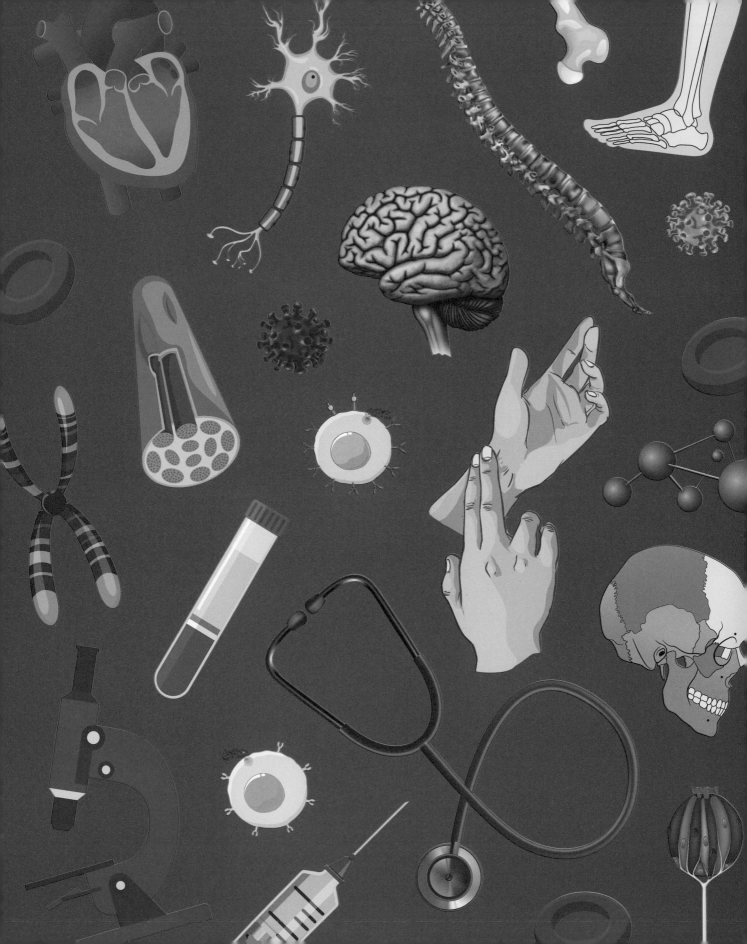

FACTOLOGY
THE HUMAN BODY
Open up a world of information!

ARE YOU READY
TO EXPLORE...

Get under the skin of the most astonishing machine you'll ever have: your own body! Discover what your different organs do, how your senses help you understand the world around you, and the miracles of modern medicine.

Let's slice into the secrets of your own biology! Where do you – and the human species – come from? What makes poo brown? How much DNA do you share with a banana? We're on a myth-busting mission to answer every question you have about what makes you... YOU! Find out about the strangest illnesses imaginable and the most curious cures, and explore the inner workings of eyeballs, brains, muscles and much else in a book that proves there's no such thing as 'only human'!

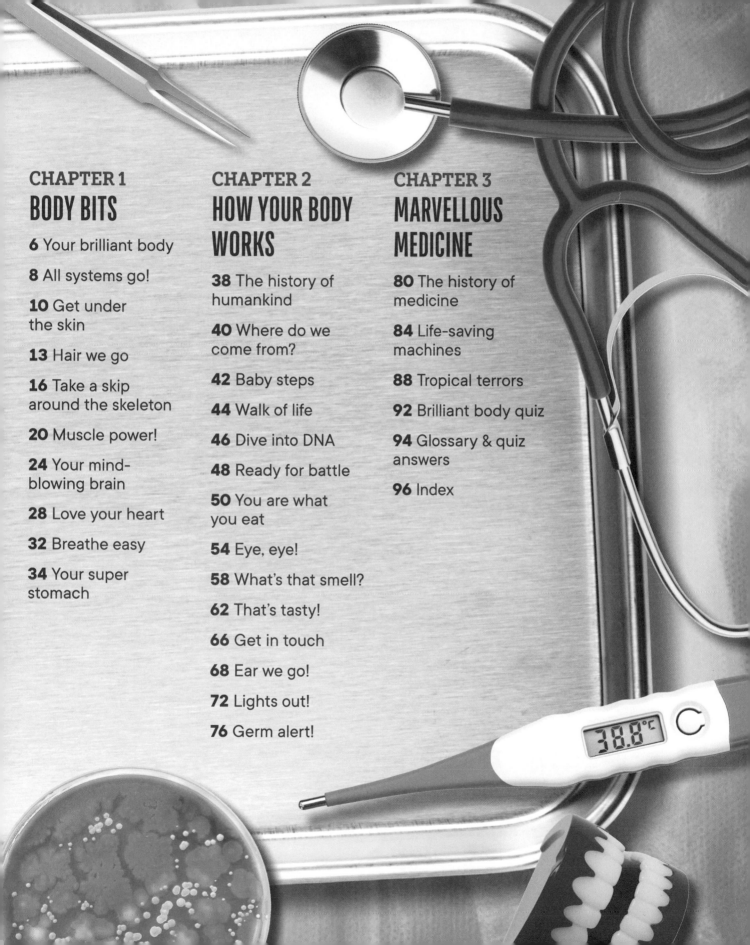

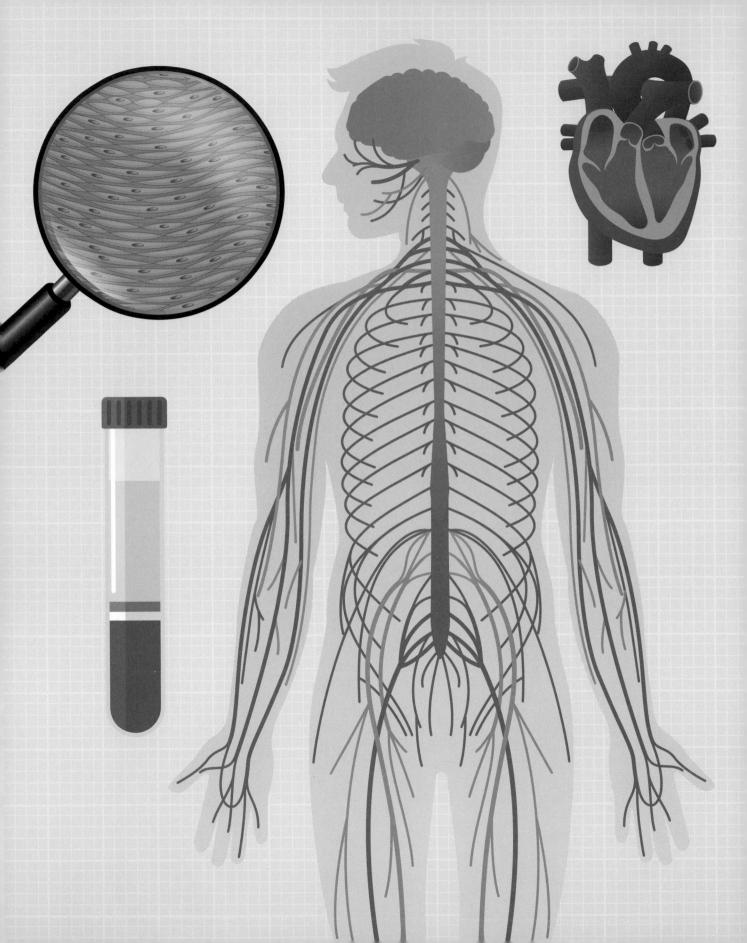

CHAPTER 1

BODY BITS

It's time to get to know the inner (and outer!) workings of your body, from its tiniest cells to the major organs, like the heart and brain. What makes your skin so stretchy? What does your diaphragm do? And how do your insides produce all that poo? Read on for the inside story...

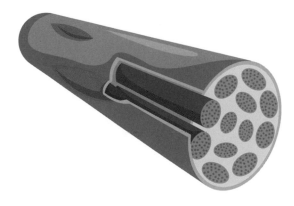

YoUr BrILLIANT BoDY

Your body is an awesome machine. All of its parts work together – from your tiniest cells to your incredible organ systems – to keep you alive and make you who you are

Elements

You're made of the same stuff as everything else on this planet – elements. There are 118 pure chemical elements that are made from just one type of atom and humans are mostly made of four of them – oxygen, carbon, hydrogen and nitrogen. About 0.00000005% of your body is made of gold!

Atoms

These tiny particles are the building blocks of everything around you. They're so small, even the most powerful microscopes can't see one on its own!

Molecules

Atoms can join together to form molecules. There are trillions of molecules in every single cell in your body!

Cells

You're a multicellular organism! That means you're made up of lots of cells – around 30 trillion to be exact. There are hundreds of different types, all carrying out specific tasks inside you every second. Blood cells are collecting oxygen from your lungs and delivering it all over your body, nerve cells are sending messages from your brain to other parts and muscle cells are helping you move around. Some last a lifetime, but others die after a few days – your body is making around five million new ones every second to replace them!

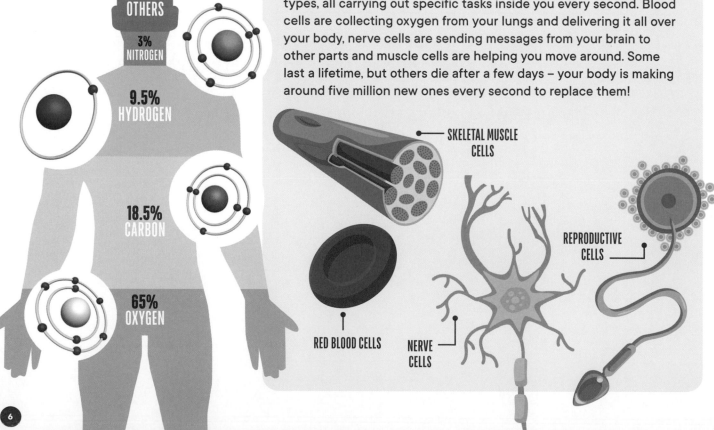

OTHERS

3%
NITROGEN

9.5%
HYDROGEN

18.5%
CARBON

65%
OXYGEN

SKELETAL MUSCLE CELLS

REPRODUCTIVE CELLS

RED BLOOD CELLS

NERVE CELLS

DIFFERENT TYPES OF TISSUE

Cells that have the same job to do group together as tissues. There are four main types:

1 **Muscle tissue** These cells are able to pull on your bones to make them move.

2 **Connective tissue** Strong, flexible cartilage helps to cushion your bones.

3 **Epithelial tissue** These sheets of cells cover and line the surfaces of your body.

4 **Nervous tissue** This network carries all kinds of information around your body.

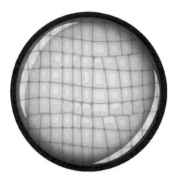 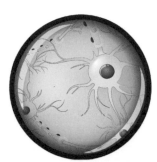  

Organs

When tissues join together to do an important job in your body, we call them organs. Some, like your eyes or your ears, are on the outside of your body, but most are on the inside. Five of them are so important that you couldn't live without at least one of them – your brain, heart, liver, lungs and kidneys. You can see the major organs in your body here.

Systems

Your organs work together in different groups known as systems – there are 11 of them. Your digestive system, for example, includes your stomach and intestines, and together they break down the food that you eat to give you energy.

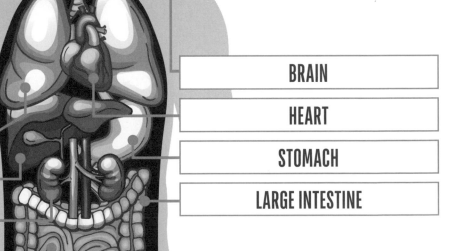

LUNGS

LIVER

KIDNEYS

SMALL INTESTINE

BRAIN

HEART

STOMACH

LARGE INTESTINE

ALL SYSTEMS GO!

All of the amazing things your body can do are carried out by the 11 systems you can see here. Each one includes a group of organs that perform particular tasks, but the systems join forces to keep you healthy and working properly

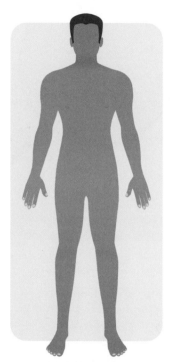

INTEGUMENTARY SYSTEM

Your skin, hair and nails protect your body from injury and infection, and store body fat

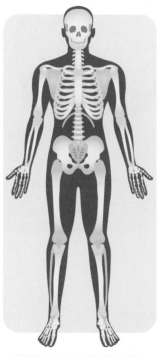

SKELETAL SYSTEM

Your bones support your body, store minerals and even make blood cells

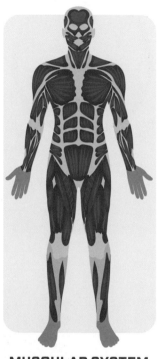

MUSCULAR SYSTEM

Your muscles allow you to move and balance

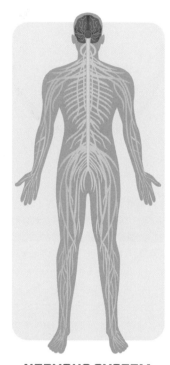

NERVOUS SYSTEM

Your brain, spinal cord and nerves control your body, sensing your environment and carrying messages

DID YOU KNOW?

All your systems work together! Your respiratory system takes in oxygen and delivers it to other systems via your cardiovascular system, helping you breathe easy.

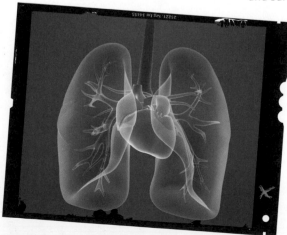

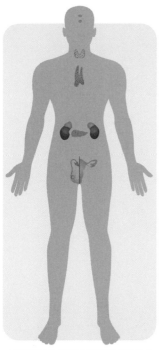

ENDOCRINE SYSTEM

Glands and tissues produce hormones that control activities like growth and reproduction

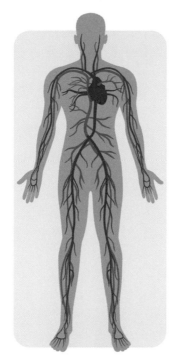

CARDIOVASCULAR SYSTEM

Pumps blood around a network of vessels, transporting oxygen and removing waste

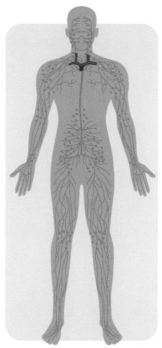

LYMPHATIC SYSTEM

Your immune system defends the body and protects all of your systems from infection

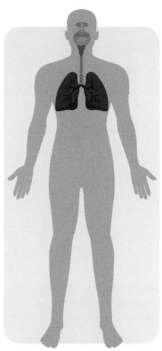

RESPIRATORY SYSTEM

Your lungs take in oxygen and expel waste gases. They also help keep your temperature in check

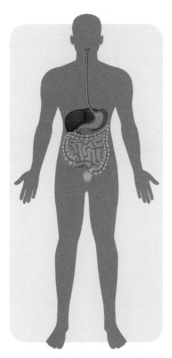

DIGESTIVE SYSTEM

Your stomach and gut break down food for your body to absorb

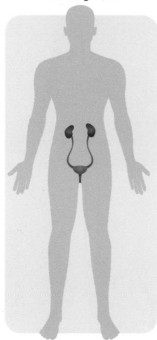

URINARY SYSTEM

Your kidneys clean your blood and filter out waste via the bladder

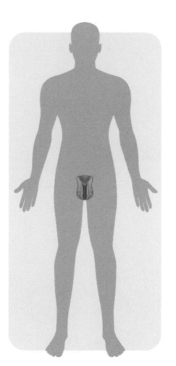

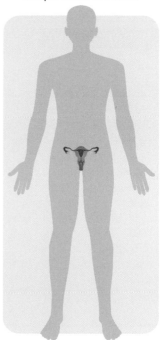

REPRODUCTIVE SYSTEM

The male reproductive system produces and delivers sperm

The female reproductive system creates eggs and can help a baby grow

GET UNDER THE SKIN

Skin is your body's largest organ and its first line of defence! Working together with your hair, nails and nerves, it acts as a tough armour, protecting you from harmful elements like germs and the Sun's UV rays. It also stops your body fluids leaking away and keeps you from getting too hot or cold! It's time to get under the skin of this amazing organ...

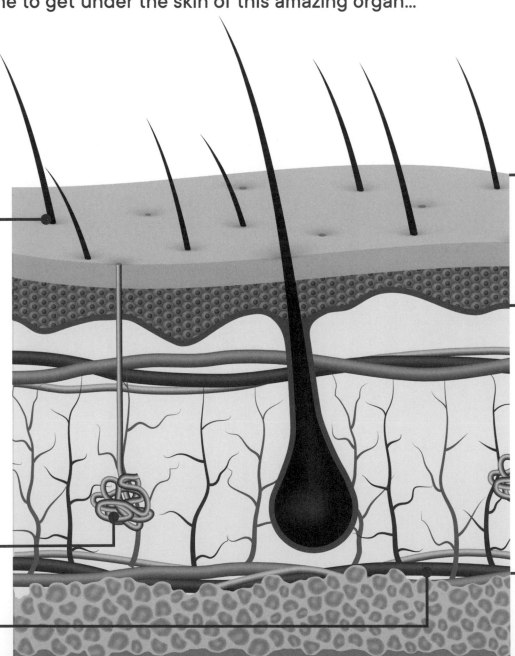

HAIR FOLLICLES

Tiny pits in the dermis layer of your skin called follicles make hair. There are millions of tiny 'vellus' hairs all over your body. While you can barely see them, they act as a blanket, standing up to trap air when you're cold.

SWEAT GLANDS

Your skin's on top when it comes to regulating your body temperature. When you're running around, sweat glands in the dermis release moisture onto the surface of the epidermis where it evaporates, helping you to cool off. It also sends signals to control blood vessels near the skin – narrowing them if you're cold and widening them if you're too hot.

BLOOD VESSEL

Pinch yourself

There's a good reason parents and guardians encourage you to drink plenty of water – it keeps your body and skin hydrated! This hydration, along with two proteins, collagen and elastin, help your skin to spring back after it's been stretched. Want to see that in action? Try this test: gently pinch the back of your hand and see how quickly the skin returns to normal. The older you are, the longer it takes!

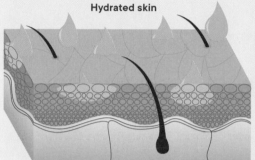

Hydrated skin

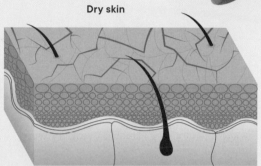

Dry skin

EPIDERMIS

This thin top layer is mostly dead! You shed around 30,000 dead skin cells every minute from the top of the epidermis, and your body replaces them with new ones at the bottom. These new cells fill up with a tough substance called keratin, a natural protein found in the body, and harden before dying, flattening out and flaking off. Every month you regrow a whole new outer layer of skin!

DERMIS

This second layer is much thicker and is packed with bendy collagen fibres to give skin its elasticity and strength, along with tiny sweat glands, blood vessels and nerves. Millions of micro sensors also help detect touch and pain.

SUBCUTANEOUS

This deep third layer is made up mostly of collagen and fat, which supplies nutrients to the other two layers. It keeps the body warm and acts as a shock absorber, cushioning it from injury.

Beneath the surface

On average your skin is 2-3mm thick – the size of a new crayon point – but different parts of your body have thicker skin than others. Touch the soles of your feet and palms of your hands– can you feel that the skin is thicker there, when compared to the delicate skin of your eyelids?

Every inch of your skin has an exact stretchiness and strength for its location. That's because they've adapted to do the job they're used for, such as walking or gripping. But like the tip of an iceberg, the layer you can feel, called the epidermis, is just the part you can see. There are two other important layers lying beneath as well: the dermis and subcutaneous.

All the colours

Skin comes in many beautiful tones and colours. Someone living in a tropical climate may be more likely to have darker skin than someone living in a colder climate. That's because cells in the epidermis produce a pigment called melanin to protect us from the sun's harmful ultraviolet (UV) rays. It's also why you develop a tan when you spend time on the beach, and why it's important to wear lotion with a high SPF (sun protection factor)!

Wrinkles and crinkles

You may have heard them called 'laughter lines' – the lines or wrinkles that appear on the faces of older people. As you age, the dermis loses collagen and elastin and your skin becomes thinner and less elastic. The fat cells that give skin its plump appearance also start to disappear, causing wrinkles to form. It's a natural part of getting older.

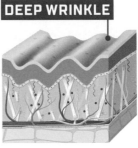

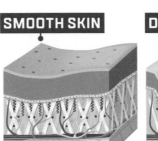

SMOOTH SKIN	DEEP WRINKLE
YOUNGER SKIN	OLDER SKIN

FAST FACTS

1. 15% of your total body weight is your skin

2. Underneath its fur, a polar bear's skin is completely black! This allows them to absorb more UV light and stay warm in those chilly sub-zero environments..

3. At less than 1mm, the thinnest skin is found on your eyelids

4. The thickest skin is found on your feet – about 1.5mm.

What's your fingerprint?

Your unique fingerprints – the swirls and lines on the pads of your fingers and thumbs – formed as you grew in the womb. They appear at about 22 weeks and will grow with you throughout your life. Why not compare yours to your friends? Dab your finger in washable paint, press on paper and notice the different patterns. There are three main types – loops, whorls and arches. Which do you have?

LOOP

WHORL

ARCH

HAIR WE GO

You might wish for different hair, but it's about so much more than what you see in the mirror. The hair on your head, for example, is thicker to keep your head warm and cushion your skull. Your eyebrows aren't just for shaping – they're designed to protect your eyes from sweat dripping down your forehead. And the job of your eyelashes is to keep your eyes safe from dust

HOW DOES HAIR GROW?

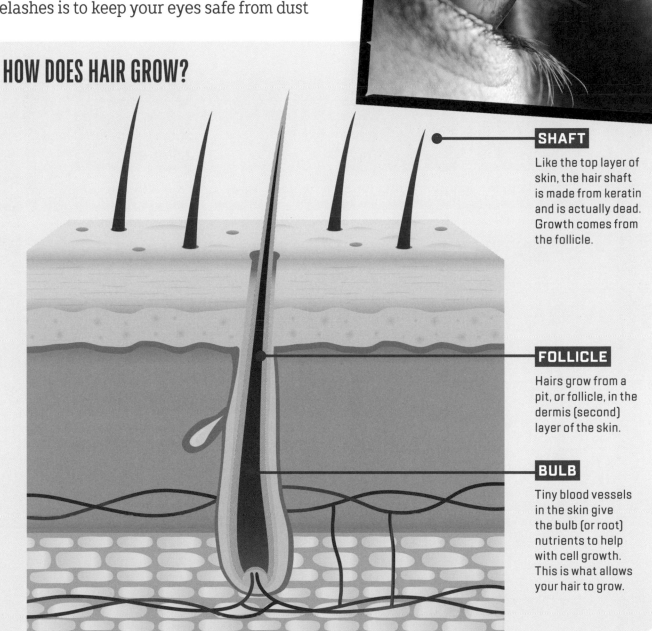

SHAFT

Like the top layer of skin, the hair shaft is made from keratin and is actually dead. Growth comes from the follicle.

FOLLICLE

Hairs grow from a pit, or follicle, in the dermis (second) layer of the skin.

BULB

Tiny blood vessels in the skin give the bulb (or root) nutrients to help with cell growth. This is what allows your hair to grow.

HAIR ACADEMY

Why do some of us have poker-straight hair and others have a head full of wild curls? Or black or blonde hair?

It's all down to your pigments – coloured substances – which contain melanin (dark brown, like the skin) and some carotene (yellowish). Your follicle shape determines the texture of your hair.

STRAIGHT RED HAIR – red melanin and round hair follicle

BLACK CURLY HAIR – black melanin and flat hair follicle

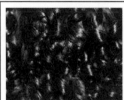

BLONDE WAVY HAIR – carotene and oval hair follicle

STRAIGHT BLACK HAIR – black melanin and round hair follicle

STRAIGHT HAIR

KINKY HAIR

CURLY HAIR

5 YEARS: THE AVERAGE TIME A SCALP HAIR GROWS BEFORE FALLING OUT

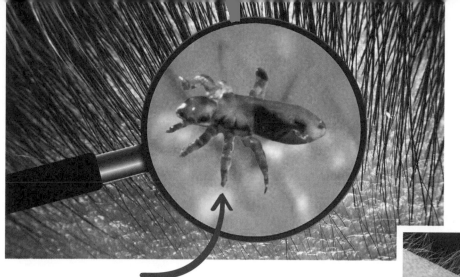

Goosebumps

Goosebumps are the body's clever way of protecting you from chills. Tiny muscles contract and make your hairs 'stand on end', trapping more air to keep you warm. Why are they called 'goosebumps'? Have a look at a plucked goose or chicken – they're bumpy too!

Creepy crawlies

Mini wingless critters called head lice (AKA Pediculus humanus capitis) love to set up home in your hair and, like little vampires, survive by sucking blood out of your scalp! But don't worry – they're harmless and a special treatment can send them packing. No garlic required!

THE NAIL FILES

Like your skin and hair, nails are made of keratin. The roots are hidden under the skin, all the way back to the nearest knuckle. Nails protect the sensitive nerves at the end of your fingers that send signals to your brain when you touch something.

Toe to toe

If you're unlucky enough to drop something on your foot and damage a toenail, the nail will eventually fall off, but not before another one has started to form underneath. It might seem gross, but you can see how the soft skin toughens up to create a new nail. You'll have to be patient, too – a toenail can take up to 18 months to grow back completely, while a fingernail takes just four to six.

No picking

American Lee Redmond holds the record for the longest fingernails grown by a woman. She started growing them in 1979, and they eventually reached a total length of 8.65 metres! We're guessing she didn't pick her nose when no one was looking...

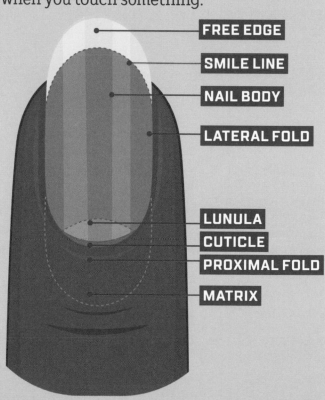

FREE EDGE

SMILE LINE

NAIL BODY

LATERAL FOLD

LUNULA
CUTICLE
PROXIMAL FOLD
MATRIX

TAKE A SKIP AROUND
THE SKELETON

Your skeleton stops your body from being a giant wobbly jelly, and it has three other important jobs too. It protects your organs, helps your body move and, incredibly, even makes blood!

Bone deep

Your bones are alive, packed with a network of nerves, blood vessels and cells. They bleed when they're cut and can grow and repair themselves. When you were born, you had more than 300 of them! As they grow, babies' bones join together to make bigger bones. Although there are different bone sizes and shapes, they share the same basic structure.

SPONGY BONE

Don't be fooled by the name – spongy bone, which makes up 20% of your skeleton, isn't soft. Its strength comes from a special honeycomb structure designed to absorb shock and protect the bones from fractures and breakages. It's found mainly at the end of your 'long' bones, such as the thigh bone – or femur – that runs from your hip to your knee.

COMPACT BONE

Making up 80% of your skeleton, compact bone forms a protective shell around the spongy bone tissue – it's what makes bones strong. It's made from proteins like collagen (a tough, bendy substance that keeps your bones flexible) and minerals such as calcium – that's the reason you're told to drink milk!

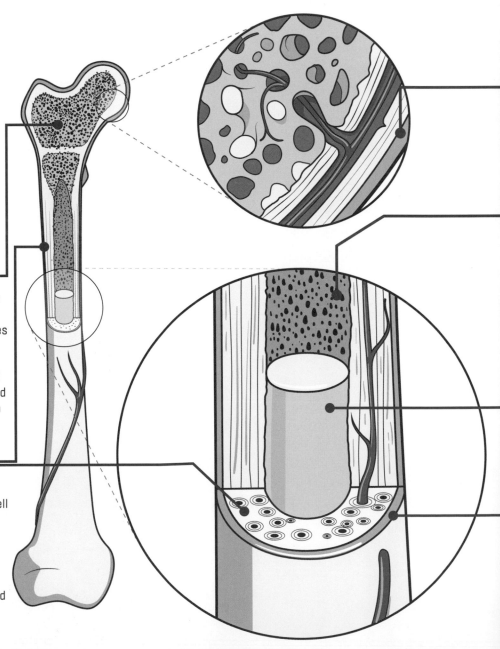

CARTILAGE

Smooth, see-through and glassy in appearance, cartilage coats the ends of bone surfaces. Without it, simple movements such as bending your arm or taking a step would hurt!

ENDOSTEUM

This soft, thin connective tissue lines the inner cavity of your long bones. If you fracture one, the endosteum comes to the rescue, creating new cells to start the healing process.

BONE MARROW

Deep within certain bones, blood is made in a fatty tissue called red bone marrow. Every day, your red bone marrow makes five billion blood cells – it's a blood-making factory! When you're young, almost all of your bones contain red bone marrow. As you get older, some of it turns to yellow marrow, which is basically a storeroom for fat. That's because your body needs more blood when it's growing a lot.

PERIOSTEUM

This tough, thin connective tissue covers your bones like cling film. Made up of two layers, it's very important for both repairing and growing bones.

How do your bones grow?

Think about when you were a baby. You had tiny hands, tiny feet... tiny everything! As you grew older, everything became bigger, including your bones. You were born with about 300 bones! Some of these bones were made of cartilage, a flexible tissue. During childhood, these eventually fuse (grow together) and are replaced by the 206 bones that a grown-up has – with a lot of help from calcium. By the time you reach around 25, this process stops, and your bones are as big as they'll ever be.

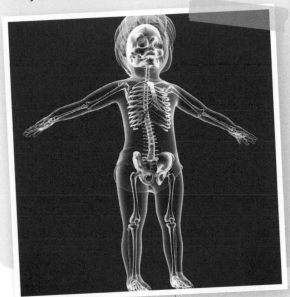

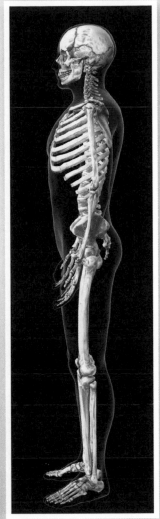

FAST FACTS

1 Bones are extraordinarily strong: ounce for ounce, they're stronger than steel!

2 The teeniest bone, the stapes, is found in the middle ear.

3 The only bone not connected to another is the hyoid, a horseshoe-shaped bone found at the base of the tongue.

4 The strength-giving structures found inside your bones have been copied by engineers in many man-made marvels, including the Eiffel Tower in Paris!

BREAKING BAD

We put our resilient bodies through a lot every single day, often without any drama. However, fractures and breaks can happen – ouch! – and the top three danger zones are the clavicle (collarbone), arms and wrist. Welcome to the danger zone!

We can rebuild!

If you break or fracture a bone, your body starts the healing process immediately. If it's a bad break, the doctor may decide to use metal pins and plates to hold the bone in place to help the process, which usually takes around 12 weeks.

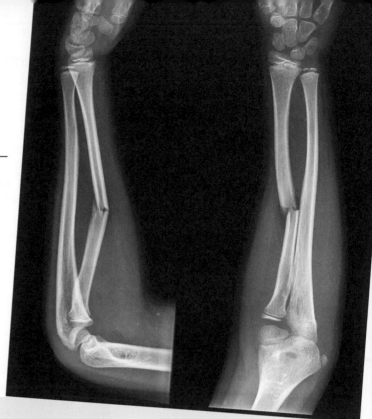

FIXING A FRACTURE? IT'S AS EASY AS ONE, TWO, THREE...

1 The Hematoma blood clot starts to form.

2 It slowly turns into a soft cartilage that keeps everything in place.

3 This starts to set and knit the bone together.

FROM THIS

TO THIS

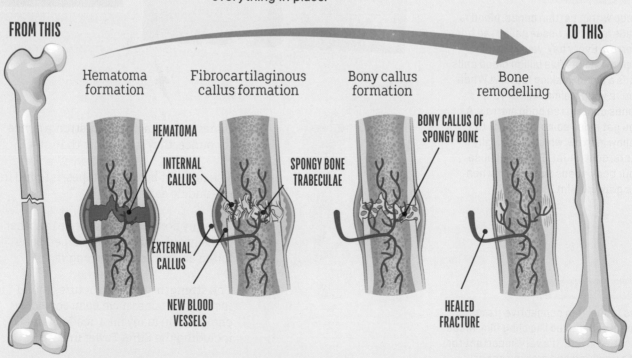

Hematoma formation

Fibrocartilaginous callus formation

Bony callus formation

Bone remodelling

HEMATOMA

INTERNAL CALLUS

SPONGY BONE TRABECULAE

BONY CALLUS OF SPONGY BONE

EXTERNAL CALLUS

NEW BLOOD VESSELS

HEALED FRACTURE

MOVE IT!

You'll find joints wherever two or more bones meet in the body and most of them are moveable – your elbows, wrists or knees, for example. But there are also fixed joints, like the ones found on your skull, which are firmly stuck together.

PIVOT JOINT This joint lets you move your head from side-to-side

HINGE JOINT Just like a door hinge, this joint lets you bend and straighten your elbows, knees, toes and fingers. You also have one in your jaw!

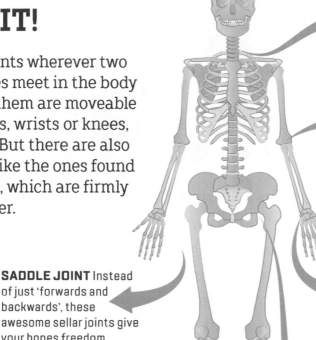

SADDLE JOINT Instead of just 'forwards and backwards', these awesome sellar joints give your bones freedom

ELLIPSOIDAL JOINT You can activate these joints in your knuckles by clenching your fists. Also found in your wrists, they create up-and-down and side-to-side movement

PLANE JOINT These gliding joints allow bones to easily slide past each other without causing nasty friction

BALL-AND-SOCKET JOINT This heavy-duty joint lets you circle your arms or stretch your leg out behind you

Spine tingler

Reach around to the centre of your back and feel those knobbly bits. That's your spine! It lets you twist and bend and holds your body upright. It also supports your head, which is one of the body's heaviest parts, weighing around 5kg (the same as a small baby!) in a grown-up. This essential part of the skeleton also protects the spinal cord, which is an information superhighway of nerves firing information from your brain to the rest of the body.

You might think it's straight, but your spine runs from the base of your skull to your lower back in a loose 'S'-shape. It's made up of 33 bones called vertebrae that look like rings. In between, 'intervertebral' discs act like shock absorbers.

Skull: Crushing it!

There are 22 bones in your skull! Only one – your jaw – can move, so you can eat, talk and yawn. The rest are locked together to keep your brain, eyes and ears protected. It also underpins and shapes the look of your face.

While your teeth are still growing and changing throughout childhood, when you grow up, you will have 32 in total. These are all attached to the bones of the upper and lower jaws.

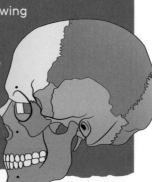

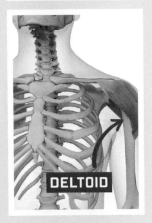

BICEPS

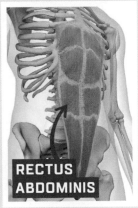

DELTOID

RECTUS ABDOMINIS

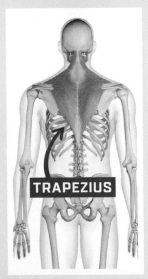

TRAPEZIUS

MUSCLE POWER!

You have more than 640 muscles in your body and they're the reason you can move – they have the power to shift the bones of your skeleton. Many of them you control, such as when you text a friend or stand up, but there are lots of other muscles – including your heart – working all the time on their own. Let's get moving!

Every muscle has a scientific or medical name. The ones in the top part of your arm are called the biceps (front) and triceps (back). Strong rope-like tendons made from a protein called collagen join the slimmer end of muscles to the surface of the bone, like super glue! Muscles are all made of the same material – a type of elastic tissue that's similar to a rubber band. Tens of thousands of fine thread-like fibres make up each muscle. Be brave and ask your parent or guardian to show you some raw meat – it's very similar to what yours look like!

640 MUSCLES

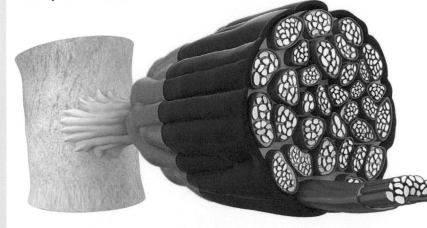

▲ Tendons connect the muscles to your bones

THERE ARE THREE MUSCLE GROUPS

1 **Smooth muscles**

Your smooth muscles mostly lie in sheets, with one layer of muscle behind the other, like two pieces of bread pressed together. But these muscles have a mind of their own! You can't control them and that's why they're known as 'involuntary' muscles. They're busy at work all over your body, especially in your stomach and digestive system, contracting and relaxing to move the food you eat from your mouth to your bottom – they're a bit like a water slide! When you need to pee, the smooth muscles in your bladder make sure you get to the bathroom in time, too!

2 **Cardiac muscle**

Your heart is also known as the 'myocardium' because it's made up of cardiac muscle, the strongest type in your body.

100,000 The number of times a human heart beats every day

9,000 litres How much blood the heart pumps by contracting and relaxing... *daily*. That's the equivalent of eleven baths full of water!

3 **Skeletal muscles**

These are the ones most of us think about when talking about muscles. They're the muscles that give you the strength and power to clamber up a climbing frame or throw a ball. You control these voluntary muscles, such as the quadricep (thigh) and pectoralis (front chest), by sending a message from your brain. They're sometimes called 'striated' muscles because they look striped. Not like a zebra, though! It's the dark and light fibres that make them appear this way, and they come in different shapes and sizes depending on where they are.

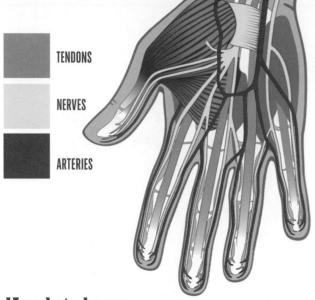

Handy to know

Incredibly, considering everything they do, your fingers don't have any skeletal muscles! While they can flex, extend, abduct (open out) and adduct (curl in), and circumduct (move in circles), finger joints are controlled by long tendons that reach down from muscles in your forearm and up from your palm. Stretch your fingers out as wide as you can – you can see that while they move independently, they're held together by an internal web of tendons and fibrous tissue.

FAST FACTS

1 Look up and down. You've just used the fastest muscles in your body! The ones that move your eyeballs can redirect your gaze in two-hundredths of a second. They might need a little rest now.

2 The word muscle comes from the Latin term musculus, meaning 'little mouse'. It could be because muscles contracting under the skin can look a little like a mouse moving underneath a rug, or the shape of some muscles.

3 Muscles make up about 40% of your entire body weight, and the same can be said for most vertebrates – basically, any animal with a backbone!

Energy store

Skeletal muscles act as a kind of energy store for your body, holding onto glucose (a form of sugar) and releasing it when needed. Essential amino acids are present, too, stored as protein. When you spring into action, these proteins start to 'metabolise' – acting as batteries for the muscles and giving them the power and energy they need to do their job.

So booty-ful!

Q: *Can you guess which muscle is the body's largest?*
A: *You're 'sitting' on it! Yes, it's your booty muscles – your bottom, your bum, your butt, your derrière or gluteus maximus – to call it by its proper name.*

You have two of these 'glutes', one on either side of your bottom. They must be big and strong to work against the force of gravity to keep the trunk of the body – from your waist up – upright. It's one of three gluteal muscles – the others are the minimus and the medius. The gluteus maximus is responsible for external rotation and extension of the hips, and you use it all the time – when you climb stairs or stand up from the dinner table.

▼ The medius moves the leg away from your body

▼ The minimus is deep in the hip and helps keep it strong and stable

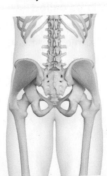
▲ The maximus is the main event – it helps control your body flexes

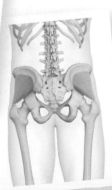

MAKING FACES

You may not think of it as a muscular body part, but your face has lots of muscles. Facial muscles don't all attach directly to bone like they do in the rest of the body. Instead, many of them attach under the skin and are controlled by signals from your brain to reveal what you're feeling. Precise movement allows you to contract your facial muscles just a tiny bit and make more than 7,000 different expressions! All around the world, people understand these 'external messages'.

CRINKLE IT
This flat muscle pulls up the eyebrow and crinkles together to make a frown

SHUT EYE
These muscles close your eyelids when it's time for bed

CHEEKY!
A smile starts here as this muscle pulls the corner of your mouth up

LET'S TALK
The muscles around the mouth help close the lips and form the shapes needed to make words

SAD CASE
When you're sad, this muscle pulls the corner of your mouth down

Try this!
Stand in front of a mirror and 'pull' a sad face. Then see the movements that change it into a happy expression. Stick your tongue out while you're there and give it a wiggle. Your tongue is actually made of a group of eight muscles that work together to allow you to talk and help you chew food.

DID YOU KNOW?
Your tongue is the only muscle in your body that's attached at just one end!

YOUR *MIND-BLOWING* BRAIN

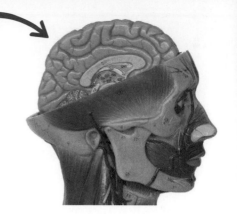

If you could crack your skull like an egg and look inside, you'd find your brain! It might look like a wrinkled lump of grey-pink jelly, but it controls everything you do. From moving, sneezing, dreaming and feeling happy (or sad) to experiencing your senses, your brain bosses your body into doing what it should be. How clever is that?

Brain power

The largest part of your brain, the cerebrum, is divided into two halves called hemispheres, and these are divided into four lobes. Its creased outer layer is made up of a thin layer of billions of cells called the cerebral cortex, or grey matter. This processes everything you sense, think and feel. Go deeper and you find the white matter, packed with nerve fibres for carrying signals.

▶ It may look like a sponge, but your brain really does soak up data. Scientists think the cerebral cortex could hold the equivalent of 2,500,000GB!

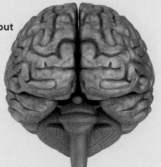

Your brain is made of 80% water, so keep it extra sharp by drinking lots of the wet stuff!

FRONTAL LOBE

Where? Behind your forehead.

Main job The largest lobe in the brain, this is home to much of what makes you, you. Your unique personality is developed here, and it also helps you understand the emotions of others – for example, if your friend is crying then it's likely that they're sad.

Side jobs Coordinating your voluntary movement, like walking or reaching up to grab something from a shelf. Helping you pay attention in class, aiding your choices about what you should/should not do, and controlling your impulses – should you really eat those 10 extra chocolates?!

TEMPORAL LOBE

Where? Behind your ears.

Main job This area makes sense of all the sound signals sent from the sensory receptors in your ears. When someone is talking to you, it's the reason you can understand the words.

Side jobs Your second-largest lobe also works to store long-term memories, like when you dropped that ice cream at your fourth birthday party. It helps with forming speech, too, and controlling unconscious reactions such as thirst and hunger.

PARIETAL LOBE

Where? Near the back and top of the head.

Main job Think about eating a delicious apple: the crunchiness, the tanginess and the sweet juice. This is the parietal lobe hard at work, processing sensory information to give you that experience. It also processes touch, temperature, pain and pressure.

Side jobs Giving you an awareness of your physical body – where all the different parts are – so you don't stub your toe or bang your head!

OCCIPITAL LOBE

Where? The middle lower back of the skull.

Main job This area is home to your visual cortex, which helps you to see. Millions of cells in your eyes send information about light, then this clever lobe transforms it into a recognisable picture, complete with colour, texture, size and distance. If you think that's impressive, it also merges the information from both eyes into one picture. Two would be horribly confusing!

Side jobs Like a speed camera, the occipital lobe helps detect motion, or when something or someone is moving near you. It also 'tells' you where you are standing in relation to things – this super skill is called spatial awareness.

YOUR **BRAIN** WOULD **FEEL LIKE JELLY** IN YOUR HAND! IT'S **CHEMICALS** THAT KEEP IT ALL TOGETHER

CEREBELLUM

The 'little brain' at the back of your head is brilliant at helping you balance, and aids your coordination – these are called motor skills.

BRAIN STEM

Where? Bottom of the brain.

Main job This stalk-like part connects to the spinal cord, which is packed with nerves constantly communicating between your brain and body. Most importantly, it controls your breathing, swallowing and heart rate, too.

Side jobs Watches your balance and stops you falling over, plus it senses how your face 'feels' – numb or hot, for example.

DID YOU KNOW?

The brain looks like a wrinkly walnut because it's folded in on itself to pack more into the space. Scientists link the wrinkles to intelligence levels! Elephants, chimps and dolphins also have wrinkly brains, while birds and koala bears' brains are smooth.

KNOW YOUR NERVOUS SYSTEM

Your body's not quite a 'bag of nerves', but it does hold thousands of kilometres of these shiny silver threads. They're your body's own internet, carrying tiny electrical pulses called neural messages up through the spinal cord to the brain stem. The brain and spinal cord make up your central nervous system, and the network of nerves that spider through your body is known as the peripheral nervous system. There's nothing to be nervous about – let's find out more…

Nerve (neuron) cells

They're funny looking things, aren't they? But the basic workings of your nervous system depend on them. The brain has more than 100 billion of these cells, many with special jobs. Sensory neurons send information from your skin, ears, tongue, nose and eyes to the brain, while motor neurons carry messages from the brain to the body.

DENDRITE
Small tentacle fibres that receive signals from your brain

AXON
The main fibre of the cell, alive with outgoing electrical signals

CYTOPLASM
A jelly-like liquid that fills the neuron

NERVE ENDING
Neurons can't pass information to each other directly. Instead, these bridge-like synapses called neurotransmitters pass the message on

NUCLEUS
The control centre of the cell

3 NERVES TO KNOW ABOUT

1 **Sciatic** The longest and thickest nerve in the body, it runs from the spinal cord to your toes on both sides of your body.

2 **Cranial** Located on the bottom surface of your brain, there are 12 pairs of these nerves, connecting to your head, neck and the trunk (top part) of your body. For example, you have an optic nerve that is essential for clear vision.

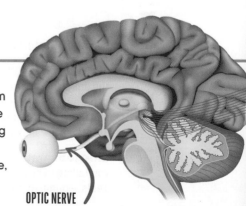

OPTIC NERVE

Two-way traffic

There are two types of nerves. First, there are sensory nerves. As the name suggests, these nerves relate to your senses. Say you touch something hot – within a millisecond a message is sent to your nervous system and you pull your hand back. Your motor nerves, the second type, go in the opposite direction. These come from the brain and 'tell' your muscles what to do. They work well together!

▶ **This is how each nerve reacts**

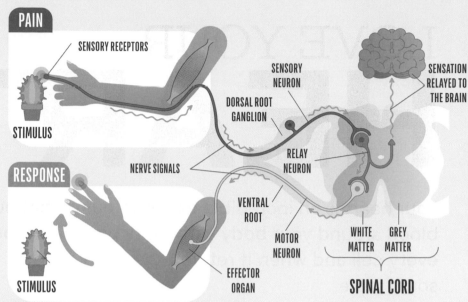

PAIN

SENSORY RECEPTORS

SENSORY NEURON

SENSATION RELAYED TO THE BRAIN

DORSAL ROOT GANGLION

STIMULUS

RESPONSE

NERVE SIGNALS

RELAY NEURON

VENTRAL ROOT

MOTOR NEURON

EFFECTOR ORGAN

STIMULUS

WHITE MATTER

GREY MATTER

SPINAL CORD

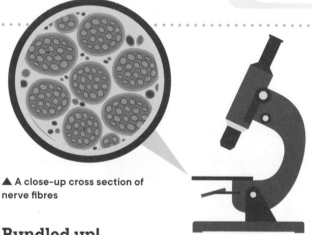

▲ A close-up cross section of nerve fibres

Bundled up!

If you were to cut into a nerve you'd see a bundle of much thinner strands called nerve fibres – you'd need a microscope, obviously! Like wires in a broadband cable, they carry their own tiny electrical nerve signals. The slowest signals travel about 50cm per second, while the fastest travel 200 times faster – more than 100 metres in the same time!

3 **Femoral** This nerve starts in the pelvis and goes all the way down the front of the leg, helping the muscles move the hip and straighten the leg.

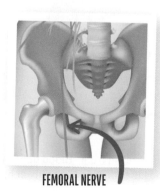

FEMORAL NERVE

Fight or flight?

You have a sympathetic nervous system which springs into action when something scary happens, preparing you for danger. Your heart beats faster to send blood to parts of the body that might need it. The kidneys release a hormone called adrenaline to flood your muscles with super energy in case you need to run away. This is the body's 'fight or flight' response. Once the danger has passed, the calming parasympathetic system takes over, helping you to relax.

FAST⚡FACTS

1 **Out of this world** There are more neurons (nerve cells) in your body than all the stars in the Milky Way!

2 **956km** That's the length of all our neurons lined up together. It would take you nearly 14 days non-stop to walk the same distance. Better pull your trainers on, then!

3 **Copycat** Why are yawns contagious? If they do help you concentrate, then it might be to make the whole team focus at once!

LOVE YOUR HEART

Your heart is an incredible fist-sized pump that pushes a small cupful of blood around your body with every beat. The blood delivers oxygen to every cell and when it returns, the heart sends it to the lungs to pick up some more

What's inside?

Your heart is hollow! Think of a balloon continuously filling with air and emptying. Inside, there are two bag-like pumps, side by side, both with two chambers: the atrium and the ventricle. These chambers are little rooms where your heart works like a recycling plant for your blood.

How it works

1. First, the heart muscle relaxes, blood flows in and fills the left and right atria.
2. These atria contract and squeeze blood into the ventricles.
3. The ventricles contract, pumping low-oxygen blood out to your lungs and oxygen-rich blood back out to your body.

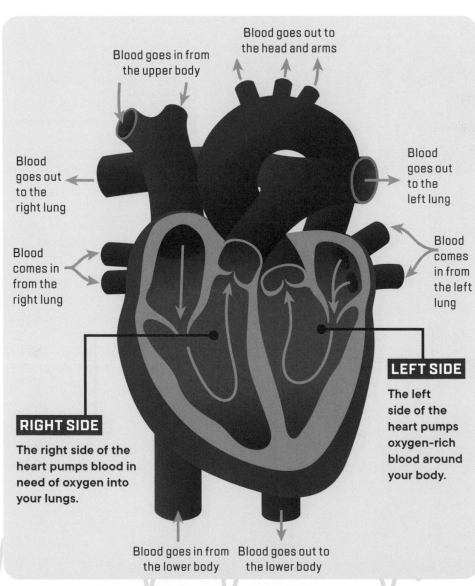

Blood goes in from the upper body

Blood goes out to the head and arms

Blood goes out to the right lung

Blood goes out to the left lung

Blood comes in from the right lung

Blood comes in from the left lung

RIGHT SIDE

The right side of the heart pumps blood in need of oxygen into your lungs.

LEFT SIDE

The left side of the heart pumps oxygen-rich blood around your body.

Blood goes in from the lower body

Blood goes out to the lower body

Beat that! The average heart beats about 100,000 times a day – which is around three billion times in your whole lifetime. That generates enough power to drive a truck to the Moon and back – a distance of nearly 800,000km! Better pack the snacks...

Heart = *love*?

An ancient Greek philosopher (a clever thinker) called Plato linked the heart to love. More than 1,000 years ago he decided that the heart was connected to our strongest emotions, including love, along with fear, anger, rage and pain.

FAST⚡FACTS

1 **180kg** That's the weight of a blue whale's heart. The heaviest in the world, it's the size of a small car!

2 **400 million litres** This is the gobsmacking volume of blood your heart pumps in a lifetime. That's the equivalent to leaving a hosepipe running around the clock for 160 days... *don't try it!*

3 **It's electrifying!** The heart has its own electrical impulse and can continue to beat when separated from the body – if it's receiving oxygen.

HOW FAST IS YOUR HEARTBEAT?
ACTIVITY

Doctors check your heartbeat (also called heart rate or pulse) with a stethoscope – here's how to make your own!

You will need:
* Plastic funnel
* Tracing paper
* Plastic tube (like hose pipe)
* Sticky tape

1. Stretch the tracing paper over the wide funnel end and fix with some sticky tape.

2. Push a short length of the plastic tube over the funnel's narrow end.

3. Place the wide end of the funnel over your heart and put the end of the plastic tube to your ear... do you hear a ba-doom, ba-doom sound? That's your heartbeat! It's also the sound of the valves in your heart closing.

4. Count the number of beats for 60 seconds. It will be approximately between 60-100 beats per minute (bpm). How fast is yours?

You can also count your pulse by placing the first two fingers of your hand on the inner part of your wrist or on your neck, just below the jawline.

SPAGHETTI JUNCTION

If you've ever cut yourself, you'll know that even the tiniest scratch can draw blood. That's because just under the surface, there's an amazing network of blood vessels delivering oxygen and fuel to all your cells and taking away waste – it's called the cardiovascular system. Let's take a closer look...

FAST FACT

96,560km The length of all your blood vessels joined together would circle the world twice!

Blood vessels under a microscope

ARTERIES

These carry oxygen-rich blood from the heart to the rest of your body at a fast rate

Super circulation

Red blood cells are a bit like cars on a road. They set out from the heart, travelling along the artery motorway at high speed. The further away they get from the heart, the smaller the arteries (or roads) become, eventually branching off into mini blood vessels called capillaries. Here the oxygen and nutrients are unloaded, before the blood slowly winds its way home along the veins, completing the journey.

VEINS

These take low-oxygen blood back to the heart at a more gentle pace

WHAT IS BLOOD MADE OF?

What's this sloshy stuff actually contain?
Let's break down blood...

PLASMA

All of the other parts float in this golden-yellow watery liquid that makes up about 55% of your blood. Produced by the liver, it transports nutrients, hormones and proteins to different parts of the body and carries waste away from cells.

WHITE CELLS

Also made in bone marrow, they keep harmful germs at bay. They're an important part of the immune system, patrolling the blood and sometimes multiplying to fight off infection. Their life span varies from hours to years and new ones are formed continuously. They're super cells!

52-62%

PLATELETS

These tiny oval-shaped cells come to the rescue if a blood vessel breaks, helping blood to clot. Platelets only survive for around nine days but are replaced by new ones made by your bone marrow.

1%
1%

RED CELLS

Billions of tiny saucer-shaped red cells make up almost half of the total volume of blood. Blood gets its bright red colour when haemoglobin – a protein molecule – picks up oxygen in the lungs.

Red cells are made in the red marrow (the spongy centre) of certain bones. Red blood cells live for about four months and are constantly replaced.

38-48%

FAST FACTS

1 **May the force be with you** Blood vessels also make up a defence system called the blood-brain barrier. Like a cinema usher, they decide who – or what – gets in. That's a 'no' to gruesome germs and other harmful substances and a 'yes' to essential substances in your body, such as water and oxygen.

2 **Blue blood** The lobster is a species with bizarrely blue blood.

3 **Ancient Egyptians** preserved (kept) the heart after death, believing it to be the centre of the body. The brain was thrown away!

BREATHE EASY

Humans need a steady supply of oxygen to live, and your respiratory (breathing) system is what makes sure you get it! Take a deep breath and get set to learn all about your lungs...

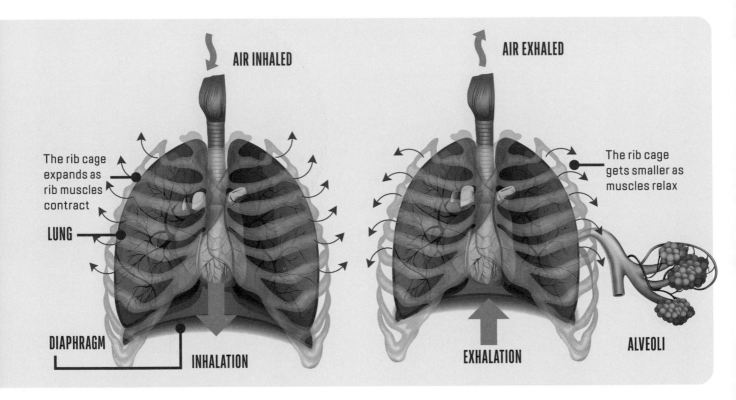

AIR INHALED

The rib cage expands as rib muscles contract

LUNG

DIAPHRAGM

INHALATION

AIR EXHALED

The rib cage gets smaller as muscles relax

EXHALATION

ALVEOLI

Breathe in, breathe out

Your body's supercomputer, the brain, controls how you breathe. Thanks to your brilliant brain, your diaphragm (say 'die-uh-fram') – a dome-shaped muscle at the base of your lungs – knows to move up and down, and the muscles between your ribs know to move in and out.

Put a hand on your chest and take a deep breath in and you'll feel your chest get bigger. This is because as you breathe in, your diaphragm moves down, your ribs move out – making the space in your chest larger – and air flows into your lungs, making them expand. Breathe out and you'll feel your chest get smaller again as the air leaves your lungs!

When you breathe, your lungs and blood swap oxygen and carbon dioxide. The oxygen you breathe in passes through tiny, balloon-shaped air sacs in your lungs called alveoli (say 'al-vee-ow-lai'). This process passes the oxygen into your blood, which whizzes it to the cells all over your body. And when you breathe out, the alveoli release the carbon dioxide!

▶ The air you breathe supercharges your blood – you are literally breathing new life into it!

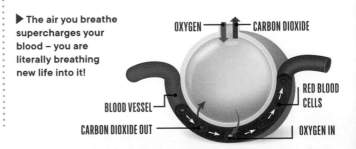

OXYGEN — CARBON DIOXIDE

RED BLOOD CELLS

BLOOD VESSEL

CARBON DIOXIDE OUT

OXYGEN IN

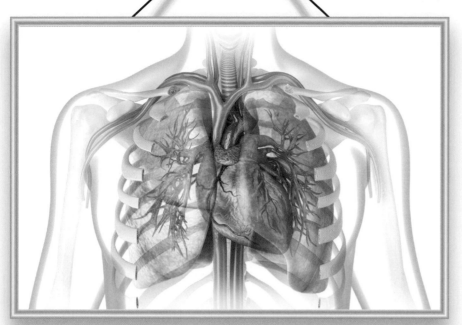

Your epic lungs!

Your lungs are a pair of spongy, pink organs that look a bit like two upside-down cones. You have one on the right side of your body, and one on the left. They're made up of different parts, called lobes. Your right lung has three lobes, while your left has two – it's slightly smaller to make room for your heart, which sits just behind.

Your lungs are protected by your rib cage, which is made from 12 sets of ribs that fit around your lungs and keep them safe.

THE RESPIRATORY SYSTEM

When it comes to breathing, you have your respiratory system to thank! It's made up of several parts...

FAST/FACT
You take around 12 to 20 breaths every minute!

MOUTH AND NOSE
These two airways meet at the upper part of your throat and are where air enters and leaves your lungs

NASAL CAVITY
This is an air-filled space above and behind your nose – air flows from your nose into this space as it's sent down to your lungs

THROAT
The air you breathe through your mouth and nose passes along your throat on its way to your lungs

DIAPHRAGM

VOICE BOX
Found in the front of your neck, this part of your throat helps air to pass into your lungs, while keeping out food and drink

WINDPIPE
This is a long, U-shaped tube that connects your voice box to your lungs

BRONCHI
These are two tough tubes that carry air from your windpipe to your lungs

RIBS

LUNGS

YOUR SUPER STOMACH

Things are about to get gross! Your next meal's about to go on a journey unlike any other – this is the story of how your food becomes poo

STOMACH

A J-shaped balloon that sits on the left side of your upper abdomen and breaks food down

SALIVARY GLANDS

These help your mouth get ready to munch!

OESOPHAGUS

A tube of muscles behind the windpipe that join your mouth to your stomach

GALLBLADDER

Just under the liver, the gallbladder supplies the bile that helps process everything you eat

1 EAT UP

Welcome to your gastrointestinal tract! When you chew your food, the 1.5 litres of saliva you make every day turn it into bolus. This gooey mass is made to be swallowed, and once it is, 26 special muscles squeeze it down your throat towards your stomach. It takes just 10 seconds for your food to find its way down there, but your body's ready to tuck in just because of the look and smell of foods. It starts to pump gastric acid before you even start eating!

2 THE DIGESTIVE TRACT

Next on the menu, it's the stomach. This is where your body starts to digest food, but what does that mean? Tubes of muscles contract and squeeze together – when it's full, the stomach can take up to four hours to work its way through your food. No wonder it takes 15% of your energy to burn through that bolus! Gastric acid gets pumped into your fist-sized stomach and starts to break everything down into creamy chyme. That's when it's soft enough to carry on.

3 SOAKING IT UP

Once the chyme is ready to go, it's passed into the duodenum, which fills it with bile and pancreatic juices. Your small intestine is lined with tiny finger-like villi which pick up the nutrients on offer before forcing the leftover chyme further down, into the large intestine. Not only does it collect the nutrients in your food and drink, but this section is also designed to kill bad bacteria!

4 LARGE AND IN CHARGE

The large intestines have some massive talents – they can even turn the liquids in your body into solid mass. Think of it a bit like a rubbish compactor at the tip! The chyme passes through this section and once your body's picked out all of the good stuff, it starts to turn your food into faeces... AKA poo. The muscles wring the faeces further and further through a collection of tubes, until...

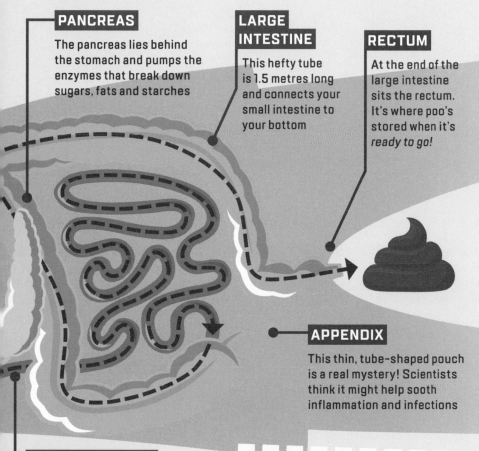

PANCREAS

The pancreas lies behind the stomach and pumps the enzymes that break down sugars, fats and starches

LARGE INTESTINE

This hefty tube is 1.5 metres long and connects your small intestine to your bottom

RECTUM

At the end of the large intestine sits the rectum. It's where poo's stored when it's *ready to go!*

APPENDIX

This thin, tube-shaped pouch is a real mystery! Scientists think it might help sooth inflammation and infections

SMALL INTESTINE

Also known as the small bowel, this hard-working organ adds bile and pancreatic juice into the mix

5 THE OTHER END

Your body's full of sphincters, and it's already used these ring-shaped muscles on your food's journey, but now the external anal sphincter is ready to do its job. This sphincter connects your inner body to the outside world by letting faeces pass through the rectum and the anus – that's the bottom to you and me! This technical process is known as defecation... everything squeezes tightly, and out pops the lump of poo. Ta-da!

Eating experiment

It's something we've all wondered: why does sweetcorn stay in your poo? The kernels are super starchy but the husk is made of cellulose, so it's hard for stomachs to digest. Why not try a simple experiment? The next time you eat sweetcorn, time your food's journey from your plate... to the toilet bowl!

DID YOU KNOW?

Why is poo brown? It's a potent mix of bile and bilirubin! Bilirubin is a chemical made when red blood cells are broken down. It travels around your body until it ends up in your poo. Want to paint one? That's the pigment!

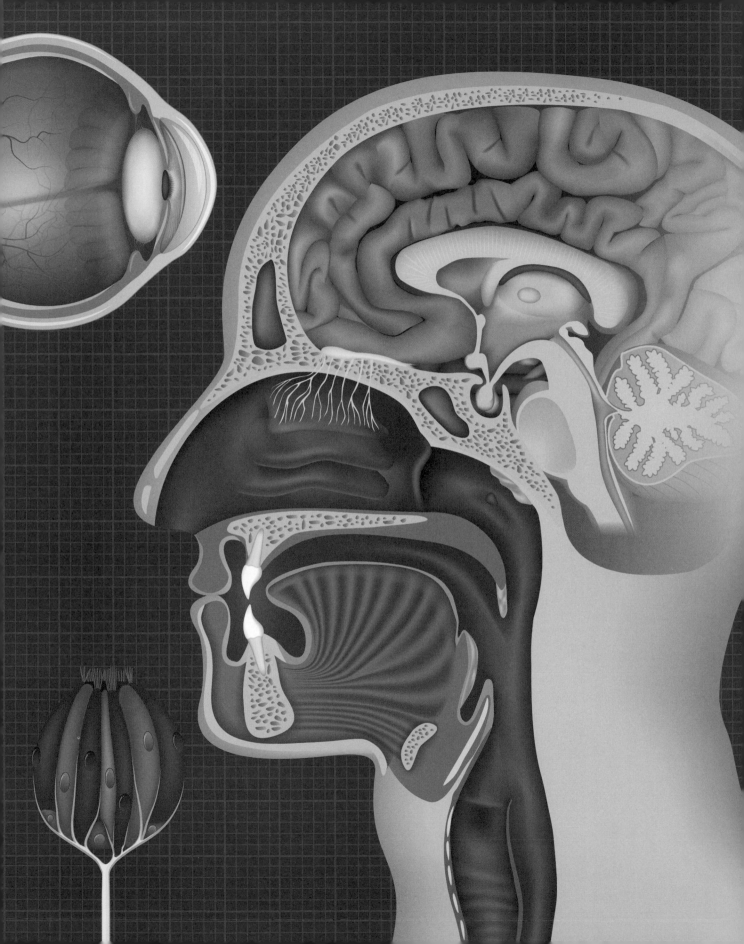

CHAPTER 2

HOW YOUR BODY WORKS

The human body is an enormously complex system. It's evolved over millions of years to let us interpret the world around us through our different senses and protect us from dangerous germs. It also changes during our lifetime, as we grow up and get older. Read on for more information about the life cycle of a human and our sensational senses...

THE HISTORY OF
HUMANKIND

It's taken almost 150 years of scientific investigation, but thanks to modern research, we're now able to understand the origins of humankind better than ever before...

Human evolution

From tree-dwelling primates to modern-day humans, our family tree began at least seven million years ago, with the human race originating from apelike ancestors. Human evolution refers to the process by which human beings developed on Earth from now-extinct primates. Most scientists think there were around 15 to 20 different species of early humans, although research is still being done to find out how these species were related and why they died out.

▶ Australopithecus afarensis is one of our most ancient ancestors!

THE HUMAN TRIBE

HOMO SAPIENS

HOMO NEANDERTHALENSIS

HOMO ERECTUS

AUSTRALOPITHECUS AFRICANUS

SAHELANTHROPUS TCHADENSIS

Humans are Homo sapiens, a primate species thought to have first evolved in Africa about 315,000 years ago. We're the only living members of what's known as the human tribe, Hominini. However, fossil evidence shows we were preceded for millions of years by other hominins, including Australopithecus and Ardipithecus. Scientists believe humans are somehow related to the extinct hominins, and also Earth's great apes. Research shows humans share nearly 99% of our genetic sequence with chimpanzees and bonobos, which suggests we share a common ancestor with modern African apes.

It's thought this ancestor existed six to eight million years ago, and the species split into two separate lineages – our early human ancestors and the species that eventually evolved into gorillas and chimps.

Early human life

Over 300,000 years ago, there was a lot more human diversity on Earth! Homo sapiens lived alongside many now-extinct species of human – such as Neanderthals – and other apelike primates, including the long-extinct Dryopithecus, and even the modern-day gorilla!

AS RECENTLY AS **15,000 YEARS AGO**, HOMO SAPIENS LIVED IN CAVES WITH ANOTHER HUMAN SPECIES KNOWN AS THE **DENISOVANS**

HUMAN ADAPTATIONS

Check out three important ways humans evolved...

1 BIPEDALISM

A defining part of being human is that we walk upright on two legs. Some scientists believe this trait – which evolved over four million years ago – helped our species become successful because it freed our hands to make tools, and meant we could carry things.

Walking on two feet isn't unique to humans, but the way we walk is – most other mammalian bipeds hop or waddle, but humans stride.

Our feet are different too. Humans use their feet to support and move their whole body, while apes and monkeys also use their forelimbs. Unlike apes, whose feet are bendier, we have strong heels, a rigid arch, and our big toe is aligned with our other toes.

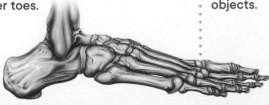

2 OPPOSABLE THUMBS

Humans evolved opposable thumbs about 2.6 million years ago when we started using stone tools more. This meant that our thumbs could be moved freely and independently of our other digits, and allowed our ancestors to grasp and handle objects.

Over time, as we learnt to make tools, our hands changed. Our fingers became shorter and thumbs grew longer and more flexible, making them much better at grasping objects.

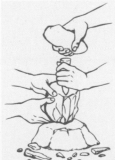

3 COMPLEX BRAINS

The earliest humans had brains roughly the same size as a chimpanzees. But between six and two million years ago, early humans began to gradually develop larger brains.

It's thought human brains grew bigger to help us meet the new challenges we faced. Bigger, more complex brains are able to process and store more information, which will have helped early humans communicate and survive in new and changing environments. Over the course of human evolution, our brain size has tripled. Modern humans have the largest and most complex brain of any living primate!

WHERE DO WE COME FROM?

You're made up of more than 30 trillion cells, but you started life as just one! When a male sperm cell and a female egg cell meet, they join to create a fertilised egg that grows to become a baby. Let's find out more about the reproductive system, which is different in males and females

MALE ORGANS

GLANDS
Glands produce fluids that mix with sperm and give them nutrients

TESTES
Millions of sperm are made here in teenagers and grown-ups

PENIS
The penis releases sperm and also passes urine

10,000 X LARGER THAN SPERM

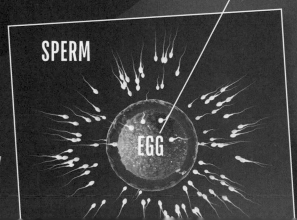

SPERM

EGG

Egg versus sperm

In most animals, egg cells are much bigger than sperm cells. In humans, eggs are giant compared to other cells in the body. They measure 0.12 to 0.2mm across – that's about the thickness of a human hair – and can just be seen by the naked eye. They're around 10,000 times the volume of a sperm cell!

Half and half

Most of the things that make you the person you are depend on your genes. Genes are stored on 46 structures called chromosomes, found in the centre of every cell.

Sperm and egg cells contain 23 chromosomes each – that's half the amount of DNA needed to make a human. When they join together, they create a zygote that has 46 chromosomes, exactly what's required for a human to develop!

MUM   DAD

SISTER   BROTHER

FEMALE ORGANS

OVIDUCT
Also called fallopian tubes, egg cells are pushed along these to the uterus

UTERUS
This muscular bag, also known as the womb, is where a baby develops until birth

CERVIX
This ring of muscle keeps the baby in the uterus

OVARIES
Females are born with about 1-2 million egg cells in their ovaries. Starting at puberty, they begin to release an egg every month

VAGINA
This muscular tube stretches when a baby is born

Facts of life

You need a male and a female to make a baby. When a sperm cell meets and joins with an egg cell in the oviduct, they form a fertilised egg cell called a zygote. The zygote moves down the oviduct into the uterus where it settles and grows into an embryo.

EGG CELL

SPERM CELL

FERTILISATION

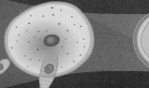

ZYGOTE

EMBRYO

BABY STEPS

No matter who we are or where we live, every human being starts off the same – as a single cell, a microscopic speck in their mum's body...

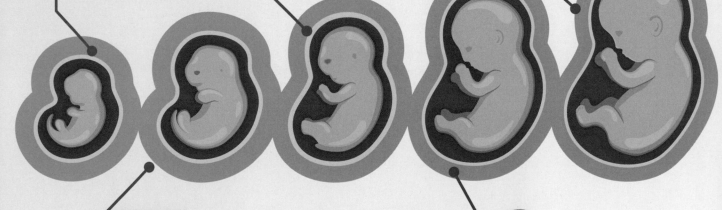

1-4 WEEKS
Once it's fertilised, the egg develops into an embryo and moves into the uterus (womb). This is a hollow, pear-shaped organ that is found in the pelvis, between the bladder and the bottom.

7-13 WEEKS
The baby's heart starts to beat after seven weeks and by the end of the eighth week, it has tiny hands and feet. It's about now that it starts to look human, bending its elbows and moving its hands. After 13 weeks, the baby is around 8cm long!

19-23 WEEKS
The baby is now able to hear, has eyebrows and begins swallowing more. It also becomes more active – kicking its legs and moving its arms – and starts to look like a mini-newborn baby.

5-6 WEEKS
The embryo starts growing and develops three layers, which will become the baby's body. The outer layer forms the baby's skin, nervous system, eyes and brain. The middle layer will become the heart, bones and muscles. And the inner layer is where the baby's major organs, such as lungs and intestines, will grow.

14-18 WEEKS
At this stage, the baby is around the size of a kiwi fruit. It starts making different expressions, begins to sense light and its taste buds are forming. The baby also has a growth spurt, doubling in weight and growing longer. Its skeleton is changing too – from soft cartilage to bone. Plus, it's possible to tell whether the baby is a boy or a girl at around 18 weeks old!

A DEVELOPING BABY'S **HEART** CAN **START PUMPING BLOOD** FROM AS EARLY AS **SIX WEEKS**

Clever connection

Babies get nutrients and oxygen from their mother through a soft, bendable tube called the umbilical cord. This cord's attached to an organ – the placenta – which also removes waste products from the baby's blood. When the baby is born, the umbilical cord is no longer needed and falls off. Everyone's left with a reminder of it though – your belly button marks the spot where your umbilical cord was once attached!

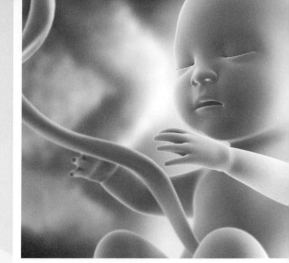

28-32 WEEKS

About the size of a pineapple, the baby weighs the same as a bag of sugar. It's developing fingernails, toenails and hair, and its body is growing bigger. The head is becoming larger too, to make room for its developing brain.

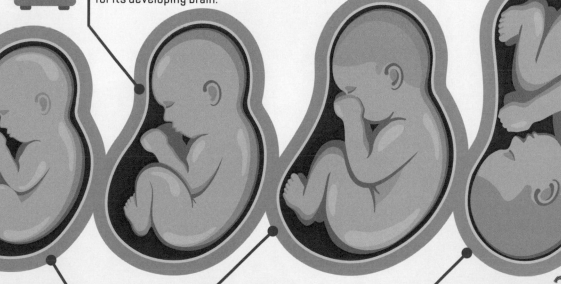

24-27 WEEKS

The baby grows from 30 to 36.6cm long and practises breathing by inhaling and exhaling small amounts of amniotic fluid. It can open and close its eyes now, and may suck its fingers – and even hiccup!

33-36 WEEKS

The baby's brain and nervous system are fully developed, and it's still gaining weight. It's curled up inside the womb at this stage, with its legs bent up towards the chest.

37-41 WEEKS

The baby is now the size of a small pumpkin! Its skin grows a strong new layer to help protect its internal organs and control its body temperature. By the 41st week, the baby is ready to be born!

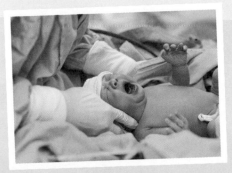

Brilliant birth

When a baby's ready to be born, its mother starts to have contractions. This is when the muscles in the mum's uterus continually tighten up and relax to push out the fully grown baby. Next, the mum helps her baby move through her vagina by pushing along with the contractions, so the baby can make its way into the world!

WALK OF LIFE

Ever since you were born you've been growing. From birth to old age, people's bodies change and develop through different stages of life. What stage are you at right now?

TODDLER
2-4 years

Toddlers change rapidly. They're busy developing language, a sense of self and greater independence.

CHILD
5-12 years

During the primary school years the brain makes lots of new connections. Children learn to read and write, test new skills and abilities and make their first friends.

TEEN
13-19 years

Known as adolescence, this is the time when children grow to become an adult. As they reach puberty, the body changes shape and teens begin to work out who they want to be.

ADULT
20-39 years

As the body stops growing, adults face lots of new challenges, making decisions about where they want to live and what work they want to do. Some people may have children of their own, too.

WHAT IS PUBERTY?

Puberty happens to all of us! It's a normal phase of growing, when you go from being a child to a grown-up.

When does it start?
It usually begins anytime between 8 and 14.

PITUITARY GLAND

What happens?

Growth spurts
When you reach puberty the pituitary gland at the base of your brain starts releasing loads of hormones. These are like messages sent around your body telling it what to do, and they're responsible for all the changes that happen to your body during puberty. For boys it means they get broader, for girls it means they grow breasts, and both grow taller and stronger.

Oily
When you're going through puberty the hormones released by your pituitary gland tell your skin and hair to produce more oil, which can make your hair more greasy and give you spots. If you get lots of spots it's called acne, and your GP can put you in touch with clinics that can help.

Voice
The hormones in your pituitary gland tell your voice box to get bigger, and that makes your voice deeper – in boys and girls!

Sweat
Puberty changes how you sweat! Special sweat glands in places like your groin and armpit start working and these produce a different type of sweat with more chemicals in. Bacteria break the sweat down and this can create a stronger smell.

Hair
Everyone gets hairier during puberty. Boys grow more hair on their face, and everyone grows extra hair on their legs, under their armpits and between their legs.

MIDDLE AGE
40-64 years

As people get older, they often have greater responsibility – at work, looking after children or ageing parents. Physical changes such as grey hair and wrinkles can start to appear.

OLD AGE
65+ years

Over 65, the body can take longer to repair itself and signs of ageing become more obvious. A good diet and exercise can help older adults stay healthy and active.

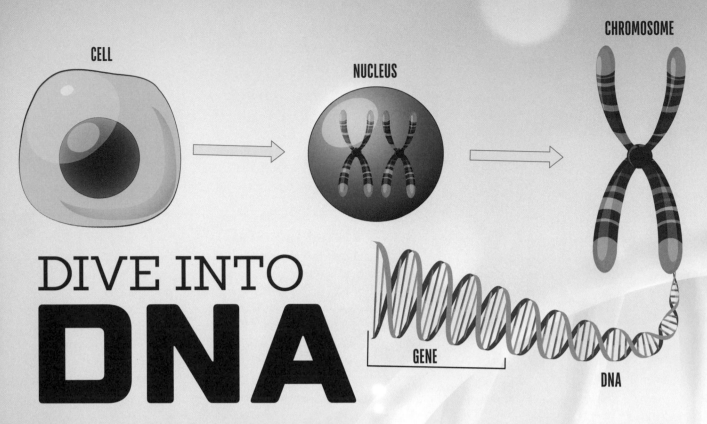

CELL

NUCLEUS

CHROMOSOME

GENE

DNA

DIVE INTO
DNA

When research into evolution first started, scientists couldn't work out why there was such variety between living things or how they passed on features to their descendants. Thanks to new technology, we have a better understanding of how things work

Clever chemicals

DNA is short for deoxyribonucleic (say 'dee-ock-see-ree-bow-nyoo-klay-ick') acid, which is a complex chemical found inside every cell in nearly every living thing. It carries genetic information and tells living organisms what they should look like and how they should grow, reproduce and function.

DNA is made up of two long chemical strands, arranged in a spiral that looks a bit like a twisted ladder. This shape is called a 'double helix' and helps the DNA pass along precise biological information to the organism's cells. The strands are microscopically thin – thousands of times thinner than a hair on your head! – and there are more chemicals in between them, which are known as 'bases'.

The order of the chemical bases is important – there are four different types and they pair up together in different combinations. Base pairs are what determine which living thing is created from the DNA – from humans to hamsters, and every other living thing!

The building blocks of life

Human DNA has around three billion chemical bases, and 99% of them are exactly the same in every person – this is why we all share so many similar traits! The other 1% is responsible for what makes you unique, such as eye colour, skin tone and body shape. Bases contain special instructions, with sections – known as genes – affecting a particular characteristic or condition. Some genes are relatively small, with around 300 bases, while others contain over one million! Each species has its own set of genes, known as a 'genome'. Their unique genome is what makes that species look and behave the way it does.

Unique sequences

We have two copies of the human genome, one from our father and one from our mother, which is why no two people have exactly the same DNA sequence. This also explains why we can inherit characteristics from both of our parents – such as freckles from our dad and long legs from our mum.

Things are different with identical twins as they come from a single egg that splits into two, forming two copies of the same DNA. However, even though twins' DNA sequences may be the same, how that information works can change over time, which can lead to differences as they grow up.

Strange but true!

Thanks to DNA research, scientists can tell that modern humans share large portions of our genome with other organisms. This is because in some ways we share similar basic functions with them.

60%
genetically similar to banana trees

98.8%
genetically similar to chimpanzees

75%
genetically similar to chickens

HOW DNA HELPS US!

Check out some of the ways that the understanding of DNA has benefited the human race...

* Analysis of DNA has helped us unravel information about our ancestors and where they came from.
* Since 1986, DNA evidence has been used to uphold justice and solve crimes.

* Understanding DNA has also changed the way some countries farm. Genetically modified crops are grown all over the world, including the USA, Brazil and China.
* DNA research has helped doctors have a better understanding of many inherited diseases, helping them predict, treat and even cure lots of them – and they're still discovering more all the time!
* Scientists have also used DNA analysis to peer back to the beginnings of human history.

READY FOR
BATTLE

Your immune system is an amazing network of cells, organs and tissues, all working together to protect your body and keep you healthy. We all get ill sometimes, but when you do, your awesome immune system fights to get you well again!

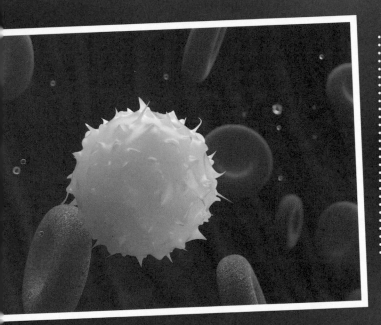

Awesome antibodies

When you run into disease-causing germs – AKA antigens – your body has an immune response. Once this kicks in, your body makes proteins – known as antibodies – to fight off the antigens.

Your immune system knows which cells to attack because it can tell which ones are 'good' and which cells are 'bad'. This is because antibodies are designed so they can only lock onto specific antigens – attacking the 'bad' cells and leaving the 'good' ones alone!

▼ This illustration shows antibodies attacking a virus – your body's a battlefield on the smallest scale!

Super cells

White blood cells – also called leukocytes (say 'loo-kuh-sites') – are an important part of your immune system. Forget the Hulk and Superman – these cells are like little superheroes floating in your blood, ready to fight off invading viruses and bacteria!

White blood cells are found in lots of places, including your spleen – an organ on the left side of your body under your heart – and your bone marrow, and they work in different ways. One type, called phagocytes (say 'fah-guh-sites'), chew up invading germs. Another type, called lymphocytes (say 'lim-fuh-sites'), help your body remember and recognise unwelcome germs and then destroy them!

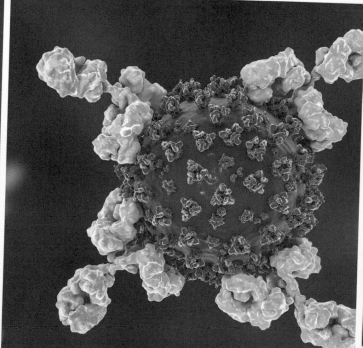

Allergy alert!

Sometimes the immune system overreacts to antigens that aren't really a threat, which is why some people have allergies. When an allergic reaction happens, a person's immune system believes something is harming them and goes on red alert. For instance, when some people breathe in pollen, their immune system attacks it, which makes them sneeze or itch.

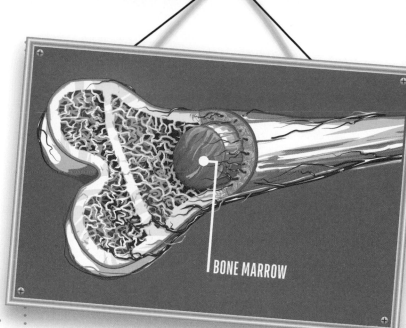

BONE MARROW

Special system

So how do your superhero white blood cells make it round your body to help fight disease? It's thanks to your lymphatic (say 'lim-fah-tick') system – a special network of thin tubes, called lymphatic vessels, that are found throughout your body.

It carries white blood cells around your body, and also helps remove chewed-up cell debris left by your super defenders, the phagocytes.

Your lymphatic system also collects extra fluid from your body's tissue. Known as lymph, this colourless, watery fluid flows from your lymphatic vessels into your blood. Lymph vessels work a bit like blood vessels, except lymphatic fluid isn't pumped in the same way blood is – it's squeezed through your vessels when you use your muscles!

Brilliant bones

The white blood cells your immune system uses are produced by your red bone marrow. This is a thick, spongy jelly that's found inside your bones. Marrow makes two types of lymphocytes...

* B Cells – these work like watchdogs, alerting your body when an unwelcome target is spotted!
* T Cells – these cells attack the invaders that have been found!

SPOTS ARE A BUILD-UP OF

DEAD WHITE BLOOD CELLS
– PUS IS A SIDE EFFECT OF INFECTION!

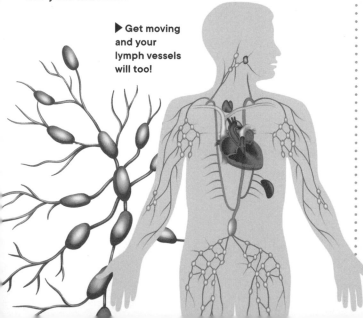

▶ Get moving and your lymph vessels will too!

Stay strong!

Want to help your immune system stay in shape? Be sure to follow our simple top tips...

1. Eat a healthy, balanced diet with plenty of immune-boosting fruit and veg.
2. Get active and make sure you exercise regularly. What's your favourite sport?
3. Wash your hands to avoid spreading germs.
4. Make sure you get enough sleep. Resting properly will boost your immune system!

ZZZz

YOU ARE WHAT YOU EAT

Does your mouth water at the thought of cakes instead of carrots, French fries instead of fruit and sweets instead of salad? Well, those treats might sound tasty, but our body needs something more substantial to keep working properly...

SUPER CELLS

It might not feel like it, but your body is constantly repairing and rebuilding itself. This is because you're made of cells that only last a certain amount of time. For instance, a red blood cell is alive for around four months, while a cell in your tummy only lasts for a day or two. So your body is always busy making new cells to replace the ones that are no longer useful – and the food that you eat affects how healthy those new cells are...

BRAIN FOOD

Your body uses 20% of the food you eat just to power your brain!

Epic energy

Just like machines need electricity or petrol, your body needs fuel to function. This energy comes from the food you eat in the form of nutrients – vitamins, proteins, carbohydrates, fats and minerals. To get the best fuel, you need to eat a balanced diet. Processed or sugary treats might taste good, but they don't have the nutrients you need to grow and stay healthy.

WHAT IF I ONLY ATE...
CARBOHYDRATES

Carbohydrates are found in things like bread, pasta and potatoes. When food is digested, your body turns carbohydrates into energy. However a diet of just carbohydrates would leave you feeling tired, craving sugar and finding it hard to concentrate!

WHAT IF I ONLY ATE...
PROTEIN

Found in things like lentils, chicken and tofu, protein can be really good for you. Your body uses it to help you build muscles, grow taller, and stay strong. Too much protein is bad news though, and would make you thirsty, upset your tummy and give you smelly breath! Yuck!

WHAT IF I ONLY ATE...
FAT

Fats help your body build nerves, stay healthy and absorb vitamins.

There are three kinds...
* **Unsaturated fats** help keep your heart healthy and are found in things like avocados, olives, salmon and walnuts.
* **Saturated fats** are found in meat and other food made from animals, such as butter and cheese. Too much of these fats isn't good for your heart or blood, so don't eat too many!
* **Trans fats** are found in things like cookies, cakes and fried food. Like saturated fats, these fats aren't very good for you.

Eating too much fat isn't a good idea and would give you a bad tummy, make your breath stink and leave you feeling worn out!

WHITE

 IMMUNE SYTEM

 PROTECTION OF STOMACH

 LOW CHOLESTEROL

 HEALTHY HEART

HEALTHY GUT

YELLOW

 LOW CHOLESTEROL

HEALTHY HEART

HEALTHY JOINTS

EYE PROTECTION

 PREVENTING CANCER

RED

 HEALTHY HEART

 HEALTHY BLOOD VESSELS

 SUN PROTECTION

CELLULAR REJUVENATION

 PREVENTING CANCER

PURPLE

 HEALTHY HEART

 HEALTHY BLOOD VESSELS

 IMPROVING YOUR MEMORY

 CELLULAR REJUVENATION

 PROTECTION OF THE UROGENITAL SYSTEM

GREEN

 PROTECTION OF THE STOMACH

 HEALTHY BONES

 EYE PROTECTION

 IMMUNE SYSTEM

 PREVENTING CANCER

Building blocks!

The vitamins and minerals we eat are an important part of our nutrition because they form the building blocks our bodies need to grow. Vitamins are good for your eyes, skin and bones, and help your body fight disease. Minerals keep your teeth and skeleton in tip-top shape, and help you stay healthy. The more yummy fruits and vegetables you eat, the more vitamins and minerals your body will have to work with!

DID YOU KNOW?

The scientific name for a rumbling tummy is 'borborygmus' (say 'bor-bor-ig-muss').

SIP SIP HOORAY!

Check out these five watery facts and find out how staying hydrated helps us survive

Your body is made up of around 60% water and your lungs are made up of as much as 83%! If you don't drink enough, you become dehydrated, which can make you feel tired, affect your mood and even make concentrating difficult.

60% WATER

90%
BLOOD

79%
MUSCLE

31%
BONE

83%
LUNGS

64%
SKIN

73%
BRAIN

You should aim to drink around 6-8 glasses of water a day – set yourself the challenge and stick to it!

Water also helps keep your body working properly by acting as a lubricant for your muscles and joints and carrying oxygen to your cells. Basically, it keeps everything running smoothly.

Got tired eyes? Water's the way to go. It can reduce eye strain!

Q: What runs but never walks?
A: Water!

People can only survive for three to four days without water!

The water in our system regulates our body temperature and helps flush out waste, like sweat and pee.

Drinking more water will boost your skin's ability to heal itself.

EYE, EYE!

Sight is the perfect syncing of your eyes and brain to make everything look fantastic. Let's take a closer look...

SCLERA
The white part of your eye is a tough outer coating that helps keep everything safe

CORNEA
A clear, curved layer that bends light as it enters your eye and directs it through the pupil behind it

RETINA
This layer of tissue at the back of your eye is filled with receptors

OPTIC NERVE
This is the cable that carries signals from the eye to the brain

VITREOUS FLUID
The jelly-like fluid that fills most of your eye

HOW DO YOU SEE?

LENS
The curved lens focuses images onto the retina

IRIS
This ring of muscle controls how much light gets in by making the pupil bigger or smaller. Its colour depends on how much pigment is in it

PUPIL
Your pupil is black because it's a hole that goes all the way through to the back of your eyeball!

STEP 1
Light rays bounce off objects around you and enter your eyes through the cornea at the front.

STEP 2
The cornea is curved and bends (refracts) the light so it enters the pupil, which gets bigger or smaller, depending on how much light there is.

STEP 3
Your lens then changes shape to focus the light onto the retina at the back of your eye, bending the image and flipping it upside down.

STEP 4
The retina wall is covered in nerve cells called photoreceptors. These cells – rods and cones – turn light into electrical nerve signals.

STEP 5
These signals are then fired down the optic nerve to your brain, which translates them into a fully-formed picture in your head.

Light control
When you're somewhere sunny and bright, your pupil shrinks to let less light through and protect your nerve cells. If you're in a dark place like a cinema, it opens wide to let in more light.

FAST FACT
When you see an image in a flat mirror, the light waves bounce straight back at you – this is called reflection. But when that mirror is curved, it bends the light rays and distorts the image – this is called refraction. You can test this out by looking at yourself on both sides of a spoon – what do you see?

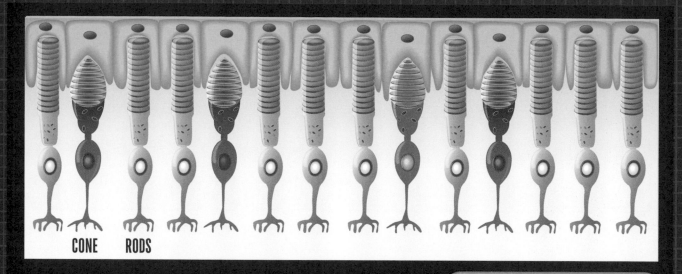

Rods and cones

The tiny nerve cells in the retina that respond to outside light are called photoreceptors. There are two types – rods and cones. Rods are tiny strands found at the edge of your retina. They react to dim light and help you see things out of the corner of your eye, while cones pick up colour and detail and give you your central vision.

CONE   RODS

ULTRAVIOLET   INFRARED

700nm   650nm   600nm   550nm   500nm   450nm   400nm

How do you see colour?

When light hits an object – a carrot, in this case! – the object absorbs some of the light and reflects the rest of it. For a carrot, only light with a wavelength of around 630 nanometres (also known as `orange´ light) bounces off. The orange light reflected from the carrot travels to your retina, where it's detected by the cone cells there.

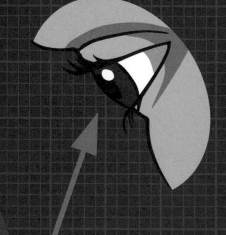

Seeing things differently

The brain works hard to see things clearly, but it's easy to play tricks on it. Even thousands of years ago, the ancient Greek philosopher Epicharmus was trying to work out why our sight was sometimes skewed. Our brains are always trying to make the simplest sense of the 3D world around us – optical illusions are artificial examples of things that make your brain go 'hmmm'.

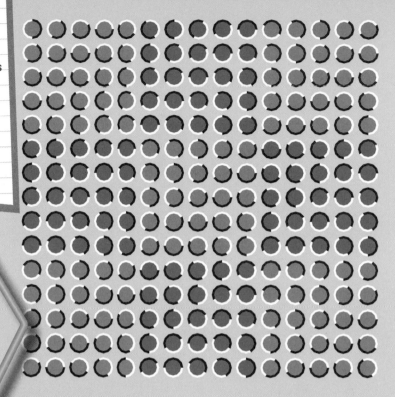

FAST FACT

Does this image look a little wavy to you? Your brain is able to take in data at 1/10 of a second – but the light source never stops. It's hard for your brain to keep up, so the information is being processed out of sync.

See the spectrum

Can't see colours? You're not the only one! Scientists think that one in 12 men and one in 200 women are colour blind! We're all born colour blind, but as our cones develop, their sensitivity to certain colours can become unbalanced. While some people struggle to spot specific colours, one in 33,000 people see in pure black and white! It's called achromatopsia.

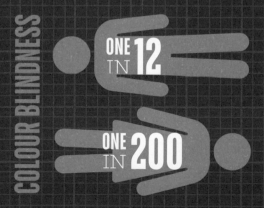

COLOUR BLINDNESS

ONE IN **12**

ONE IN **200**

COLOUR TEST

What numbers do you see in the circles above? If it's not 7, 13, 8 and 12, you may see colours differently

WHAT'S THAT SMELL?

Welcome to the olfactory, where smells are made! The hairy hallways of your nose are designed to help you decide if something's safe to eat and will taste good

FRONTAL SINUS

The gunky sinus stops your nose from drying out. When you get a cold, you'll feel it here

OLFACTORY BULB

The last space where smell chemicals are processed before being sent to the brain

SEPTAL OLFACTORY NERVES

20 bundles of smell-sensing odourants root up through the skull to send signals to the brain

NASAL PASSAGES

Your nasal passages have two roles – to carry smells and filter them

VESTIBULE

This is where smells start! When you sniff, chemicals come in here

HOW DO YOU SMELL?

Your sense of smell is called **OLFACTION** and it starts with little hair-like structures inside you called **CILIA**.

MICROSCOPIC CILIA

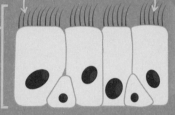

When we **SNIFF** through our nostrils, odour molecules set off the sensitive cilias.

These reactions race to hit the **OLFACTORY BULBS** and then are transmitted to their own sectors in the brain.

Smells might start off in your nose, but it's your **BRAIN** that decides if they're fresh or not!

Now you're stinking

Everybody has their own signature scent, and scientists think it takes humans back to a much simpler time. How you smell can indicate if you're ill, and one study says a meaty diet can even make you smell better! No matter how you might smell, keeping clean isn't just good for everyone around you – it can have a positive impact on your health too.

But is it off?

Bad smells are vital in nature to help humans decide if something is safe to eat, but can our sense of smell be 'off' too? We all smell slightly differently, but people cursed with a disorder called cacosmia only pick up on the worst smells – even the best aromas are perceived as pongs by cacosmia sufferers!

Smelly memories

Can smells trigger memories? When something smells, it kick-starts the cerebral cortex, where humans process language and judgement. On their way to becoming smells, these chemicals travel to the limbic system, where we store long-term memories. The limbic system crosses wires with the emotional centre of the brain, so smells often overlap with the memories your brain wants to remember.

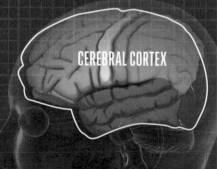

CEREBRAL CORTEX

LIMBIC SYSTEM

OLFACTORY BULB

Tasty together

Many bodily functions work together – and you certainly wouldn't have taste without smell. In fact, this super sense is 10,000 times stronger than taste! Want to test that out? Next time you're eating your favourite food, pinch your nose and you'll notice the taste drain away.

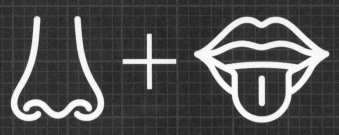

You smell different

Do we each experience things differently? It's a fascinating question and the answer is... well, it's mixed! Your olfactory receptors are doing a LOT of hard work. Depending on strong things you have smelt in the past, you have a different array of olfactory receptors on duty. This might not make you smell cabbage when somebody else smells chocolate, but your experience of certain scents could be weaker or stronger than someone else's. Weird!

The smell of rotten meat might upset our stomachs, but insects love it! The floral king of the stink is the Titan Arum – the Corpse Flower – and it uses its pong to attract bees and beetles who flock to lay eggs and fertilise it.

The stinky Eastern Skunk Cabbage attracts flies but it also has another purpose: it treats asthma, epilepsy and rheumatism. It'll help you breathe, but you may not want to!

NATURE'S WORST STINKERS

Your nose has a good way of sniffing out when something's off. Animals like the skunk have figured out that causing a stink will send predators running.

The bombardier beetle sprays toxic, boiling chemicals at enemies!

1 A total lack of smell is called anosmia. In our modern world it's not so dangerous, but imagine not being able to smell freshly baked bread!

2 Unlike some other senses, smell completely shuts down when you sleep.

3 Scientists are working hard to make a digital version of the 'olfactory code' so we can better compare people's different smell palates.

Foulest fruit

Never heard of the durian? Just be glad you haven't smelt it! It's a fruit so smelly that it's been compared to sewage and even sweaty gym socks. Eurgh! Its intense chemicals might be bad for the nose, but people believe it's a super-fruit that can cure anything from high blood pressure to getting rid of parasites. One smell, and the skin-dwellers simply jump overboard.

ACTIVITY

SMELL-OFF!

Grab seven smelly things and get a friend or family member to do the same. Put on blindfolds and try to guess each other's scents. Whoever sniffs out the most pongy points wins!

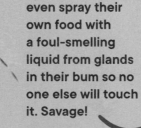

Wolverines will even spray their own food with a foul-smelling liquid from glands in their bum so no one else will touch it. Savage!

The shield beetle is known as the stink bug in other countries for a reason!

THAT'S TASTY!

You've got great taste! Welcome to the gustatory section, where we spill the beans on how your tongue works. It might look rather alien, but it's covered in dots that make things delicious!

There are **FOUR** types of papillae in your mouth, and they all work as one to help you taste and feel your food – **fungiform**, **circumvallate**, **foliate** and **filiform**.

CIRCUMVALLATE PAPILLAE

Eight to 12 of these large round papillae sit at the back of the tongue and are home to hundreds of taste buds

FOLIATE PAPILLAE

These small folds are covered in hundreds of taste buds. They're located on the sides of the tongue towards the back

FUNGIFORM PAPILLAE

Between 200 and 400 of these mushroom-shaped papillae are found at the tip and edges of your tongue. Each one contains three to five taste buds

FILIFORM PAPILLAE

These fine, cone-shaped papillae are the most common, and they don't contain any taste buds – they're responsible for the sensation of touch

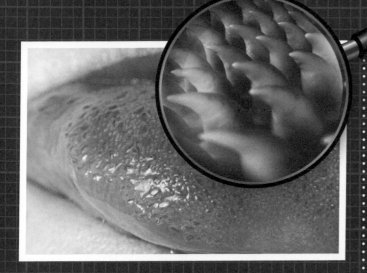

Best buds

Could taste be the best sense? Just like smell, you can enjoy it, but the tongue's main job is to keep you safe. You might think the tongue is smooth, but it's actually covered in thousands of tiny bumps called papillae. Many of these diddy domes contain taste buds – when we eat, chemicals from food called tastants are picked up by papillae, which tickle our nervous receptors. These send signals letting the brain know when food's good to eat.

A real mouthful

You can have anywhere between 2,000 and 10,000 taste buds, and they don't just sit on your tongue – they line your whole mouth. They're nestled at the back of your throat, on the epiglottis (that flap of flesh you can feel at the back of your mouth) and in your sinuses. They die off and regrow every two weeks, although as you get older less are replaced.

TYPES OF TASTE

There are five basic tastes – sweet, sour, bitter, salty and umami.

SWEET

Encourages us to eat carbohydrates for energy.

SOUR

Helps the tongue test for toxic substances and the ripeness of fresh foods.

SALTINESS

Keeps a lid on how much water is sloshing around inside us.

BITTER

Sensing bitterness stops us from eating poisonous things.

UMAMI

Rewards us for eating tasty growth-boosting amounts of protein.

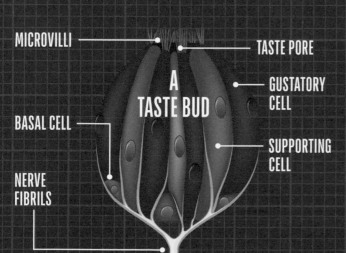

MICROVILLI
TASTE PORE
A TASTE BUD
GUSTATORY CELL
BASAL CELL
SUPPORTING CELL
NERVE FIBRILS

It's a myth that your tongue has patches that pick up specific flavours. All taste buds can detect the five types of taste, no matter where they're located!

WET WORKS

You might think saliva's just there to help you chew your food, but it does so much more. This slimy substance mixes with your food to create an easily swallowed ball called a bolus, but it also keeps things clean in your mouth and kills bad bacteria. If you think about the explosion of taste as a chemical reaction, the litre of saliva that you produce a day is the fuse that starts the process off.

Swallowing sends the bolus ball on its way down to the stomach. Rhythmic muscle movements turn your oesophagus into a tunnel and they contract behind the bolus to make sure food can only go one way. The larynx in your throat pulls upward to close the door and ensure your lunch doesn't end up in your lungs – breathing a bolus would be very bad!

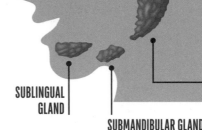

Most people make enough spit in their lifetime to fill almost 53 bathtubs. Yuck!

SUBLINGUAL GLAND

SUBMANDIBULAR GLAND

PAROTID GLAND

Give your glands a hand! These fleshy patches churn out 30ml of spit every hour.

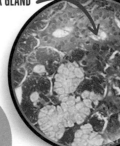

▲ Microscopic image of the submandibular gland below the jaw

1

BOLUS

2

3

4

FAST⚡FACTS

1 Swallowing's a reflex, but that hasn't stopped people training to trick it! Sword swallowers convince their gastrointestinal muscles to stay open all the way down... Don't try this at home!

2 Think you eat quickly? British-born Leah Shutkever holds the world record for eating a whole Chocolate Orange in just 57.14 seconds!

3 Your tongue is covered in a biofilm of sticky bacteria. Time to give it a clean!

Talking and tasting

The tongue isn't just for tasting – it's a vital tool for talking too. When talking, you use the same set of stimuli as touch and the filiform papillae on your tongue play a big part. Your mouth doubles as a member of the resonatory system, harnessing the wind power of your breath and voice box to shape sounds with your lips, teeth and tongue. It's called articulation – just don't do it while you're eating!

O

L

TH

anisyl formate   **butyric acid**

Taste trickery

Ever had a strawberry milkshake and wondered where the strawberries were? Today, scientists make their own flavourants – artificial versions of flavours. It's a practice that food fanatics have been experimenting with for thousands of years in a bid to trick our brains. Flavour is a chemical reaction, and from the back of a packet, you'll find a host of unusual ingredients and numbers designed to make things tasty. Scientists even used to make flavours stronger using the gland from a beaver's bottom!

amyl acetate

amyl butyrate

Nice and spicy!

Can you handle the heat? The challenge of chewing on spicy foods is enough to make anyone cry. Why? They're filled with a chemical called capsaicin that binds to a receptor on your tongue that normally reacts to heat. Your body thinks there's something hot in your mouth and tries to cool you down– hence that runny nose and red face!

TONGUE TWISTER CHALLENGE

Make the most of this moist muscle and see if you can say each of these in one go without tripping up your tongue...

1 She sells sea shells by the seashore.

2 How much wood would a woodchuck chuck if a woodchuck could chuck wood? He'd chuck as much as a woodchuck could, if a woodchuck could chuck wood!

3 Peter Piper picked a peck of pickled peppers. A peck of pickled peppers Peter Piper picked. If Peter Piper picked a peck of pickled peppers, where's the peck of pickled peppers Peter Piper picked?

4 Of all the felt I ever felt, I never felt a piece of felt which felt as fine as that felt felt, when first I felt that felt hat's felt.

5 Two tiny timid toads trying to trot to Tarrytown.

GET IN TOUCH

Touch was the first sense you developed! Millions of tiny nerve cells in your skin called touch receptors are reacting to the world around you right now. Depending on their type, they can sense if something's hot or cold, ticklish or pressing on your skin. Let's find out more about how you feel

YOUR SKIN MAGNIFIED

It may look simple on the surface, but your skin is a super-shield that protects all of your inside organs from the outside world!

FREE NERVE ENDINGS

These detect pain and temperature

MEISSNER'S CORPUSCLES

These sense very light touches, like a feather

PACINIAN CORPUSCLES

These feel all sorts of vibrations and deep pressure stimuli

RUFFINI'S CORPUSCLES

These feel your skin stretching, squeezing and pinching

MERKEL'S DISCS

These react to light pressure, like pressing a finger to your lips

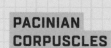

EPIDERMIS

DERMIS

SKIN LAYERS

All in your head

The part of your brain that receives and processes information from your touch receptors is called the somatosensory cortex. Imagine it as a banana shape on the top of your brain – it picks up the slightest sensations from your entire body. As Harry here is about to show you, some parts of your body are more sensitive than others because they have more receptors.

HELLO, I'M
HARRY HOMUNCULUS

◀ Scientists call this model a homunculus, or 'little man'. It shows you how sensitive your body parts are according to their size. So, the very sensitive hands and lips are shown much bigger than the less sensitive back and feet.

How do you feel?

When you touch something, the receptors under that area of skin react. They send signals to neurons in your spinal cord, which forwards the information to your brain for processing. Occasionally, though, when the receptors detect something that could hurt or damage your body, the spinal cord steps in to process the information in double-quick time.

Imagine for a moment that your finger has touched something hot. Instead of waiting for your brain to realise what's happened and move your hand away, the spinal cord takes over and flexes your muscles automatically. This is known as a 'reflex' action. It explains why sometimes you move your hand before you've even realised that it hurts!

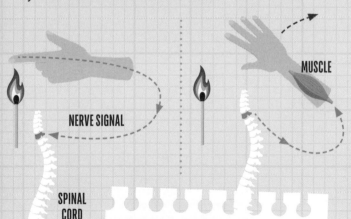

MUSCLE

NERVE SIGNAL

SPINAL CORD

DID YOU KNOW?

The reaction time in humans for touch is super speedy at just 0.15 seconds, nearly half the time for visual stimulus at 0.25 seconds

Hot air

If a normal body temperature is 37°C, why does that temperature feel so scorching on a sunny day? When your body and its surroundings are at the same temperature, heat transfer between the two can't take place, so your body can't get rid of its excess heat!

37°C

Chilling out

When it's cold outside, your body goes into lockdown. Your skin sensors sound the alarm, causing your blood vessels to tighten and slow down the delivery of heat to the skin. This causes your fluids to head inwards – it's why you might suddenly need the loo!

EAR WE GO!

How exactly does hearing work?
You might not be able to feel it, but
your ears are always vibrating in
tiny patterns that your brain pieces
together to make sound

1 Your outer ear works like a shell-
shaped microphone, funnelling
sound waves down a narrow
tube called the EAR CANAL until
they reach the body's very own tiny
instrument: the EARDRUM.

What is sound?

When you make a sound – a clap, for example – it makes the
tiny particles in the air around your hands vibrate. They then
make the particles next to them vibrate, and the sound is
passed on from one set of particles to the next in what we call
a sound wave. When the wave reaches your ear, the vibrating air
particles cause your ear drum to vibrate. The harder you clap, the
bigger the vibrations and the louder the sound.

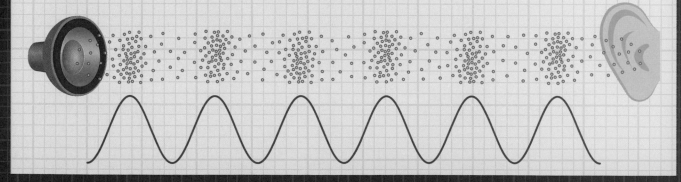

3 The tiny bones in your middle ear boost the vibrations and send them to your fluid-filled COCHLEA, or inner ear. Here, they're picked up by 15,000 fine hair cells which turn them into electrical signals.

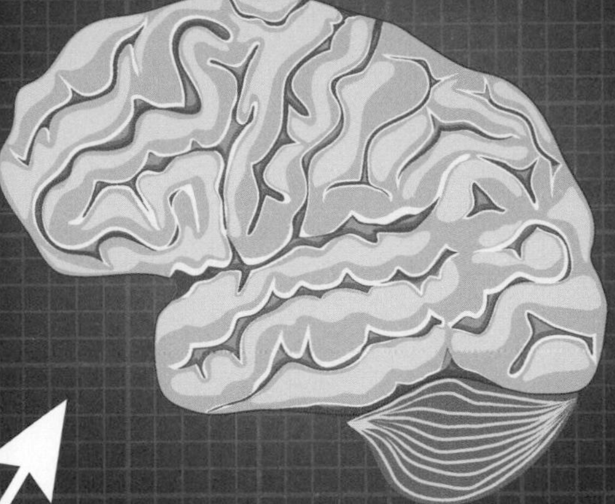

STAPES

COCHLEA

INCUS

MALLEUS

4 The COCHLEAR NERVE transmits the electrical signals to your brain, which makes sense of them.

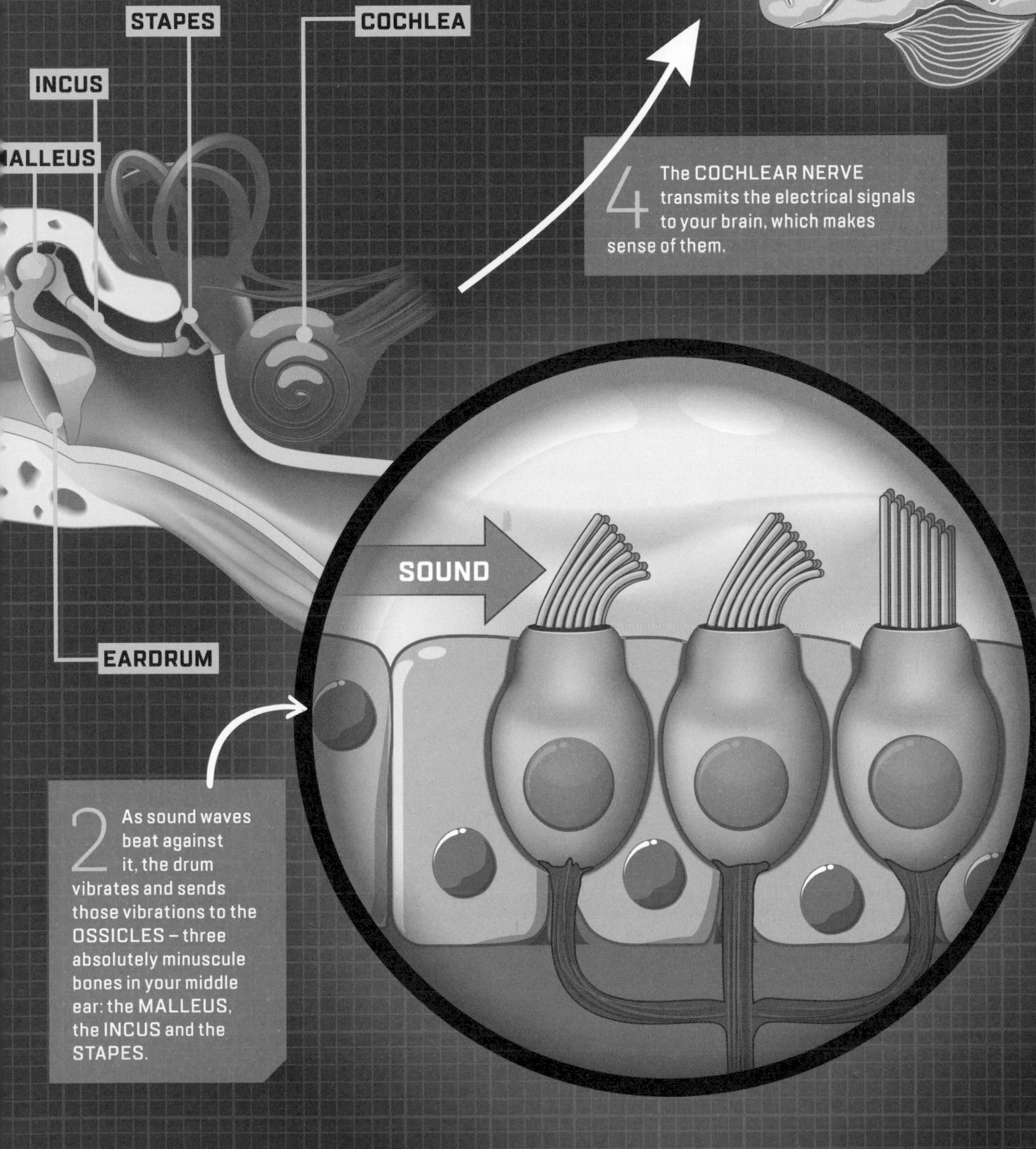

SOUND

EARDRUM

2 As sound waves beat against it, the drum vibrates and sends those vibrations to the OSSICLES – three absolutely minuscule bones in your middle ear: the MALLEUS, the INCUS and the STAPES.

Your incredible ears can hear everything from the slightest whisper to the boom of a volcanic explosion. The loudness of a sound is measured in decibels (dB). Your ears are designed to hear things safely at 75dB – that's as loud as a vacuum cleaner. Listening to louder noises for longer can be harmful.

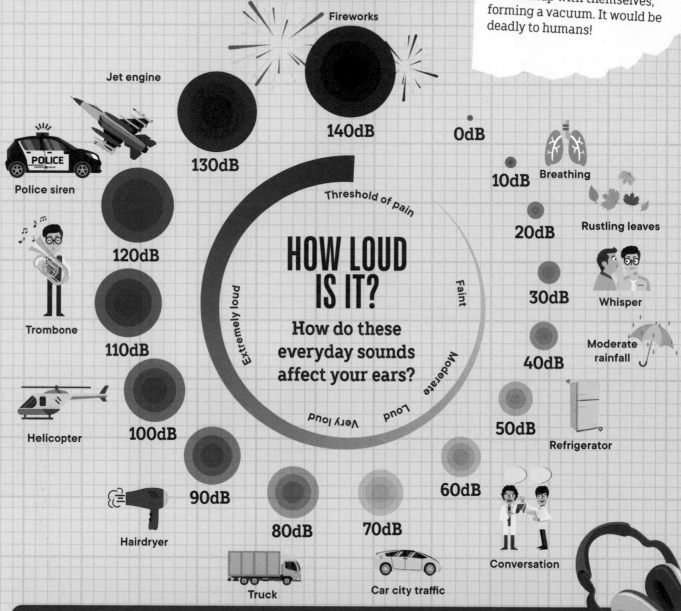

HOW LOUD IS IT?

How do these everyday sounds affect your ears?

Fireworks — 140dB
Jet engine — 130dB
Police siren — 120dB
Trombone — 110dB
Helicopter — 100dB
Hairdryer — 90dB
Truck — 80dB
Car city traffic — 70dB
Conversation — 60dB
Refrigerator — 50dB
Moderate rainfall — 40dB
Whisper — 30dB
Rustling leaves — 20dB
Breathing — 10dB
0dB

Threshold of pain
Extremely loud
Very loud
Loud
Moderate
Faint

Keep it quiet

How can you protect your hearing? Stay away from loud noises that last for too long! We have evolved to handle the noises of the natural world, but humans have invented some seriously loud technology – from 120dB concerts that can leave your ears ringing to a jet engine taking off at over 130dB. Scientists think that just 7.5 minutes of repeated sound can start to harm the hairs in your ear, so keep it down!

Pitch perfect

How high or low-pitched a sound is (its frequency) is measured in hertz (Hz). Most adults can hear sounds at frequencies from about 20Hz (a deep, bass sound) up to 20,000Hz (so high-pitched it can hurt your ears), but this tends to get lower as you get older. Anything above 20,000Hz is called ultrasound, while anything lower than 20Hz is called infrasound. Some animal species can hear ultrasound (bats), while some rely on infrasound (whales) instead.

0HZ **16HZ** **20,000HZ**

Nature's noise

When it comes to hearing, we've got nothing on the greater wax moth. This interesting insect can hear at frequencies of up to 300,000Hz – that's 15 times higher than humans! It helps the great wax moth stay one flap ahead of its main predator, the bat. Bats are famously good hearers and even use their squeaks to bounce sound waves around so that they can find their way in the dark.

So irritating!

Hate the sound of other people eating? A condition called **misophonia** makes some people get angry at sounds made by others, and it can make getting on with people tricky!

LIGHTS OUT!

We spend almost a third of our lives asleep and can't survive without it. But why is snoozing so important? And how does it help us? Read on to find out...

ZZZz

Brain game

Like all animals, us humans need sleep to stay healthy. Being busy when we're awake means our brains have lots of information to process. When we're asleep our noggins go into repair mode – which helps our brains reorganise memories and flush out toxins.

Our immune system works best when we sleep too, so snoozing also lets our body recharge and fight off illness. This is why a good sleep leaves us feeling refreshed when we wake up!

DID YOU KNOW?

A lack of sleep means that our brain can't function properly and it can affect our ability to concentrate, think clearly and remember things.

Sleep science

Research has revealed we all have an internal 'body clock' that helps us know when we should feel tired and ready for bed, or refreshed and ready to wake up. This special clock works on a 24-hour cycle known as the circadian rhythm.

Our circadian rhythm is influenced by light. Even when we're snoozing, our brain can tell when our eyes are exposed to natural or artificial light, which helps it work out whether it's day or night. As natural light disappears at the end of the day, our brain starts creating a chemical called melatonin. This chemical builds up in our body and makes us feel more and more drowsy, until we know that it's time for bed.

Our brain also produces a chemical called adenosine, which increases through the day, slowing down brain activity and making us feel increasingly sleepy. Once we've fallen asleep, the adenosine breaks down and the cycle starts all over again. Our brain eventually stops releasing melatonin during the night, and starts producing a chemical called cortisol instead. This builds up in our body and helps us wake up, feeling energised and alert!

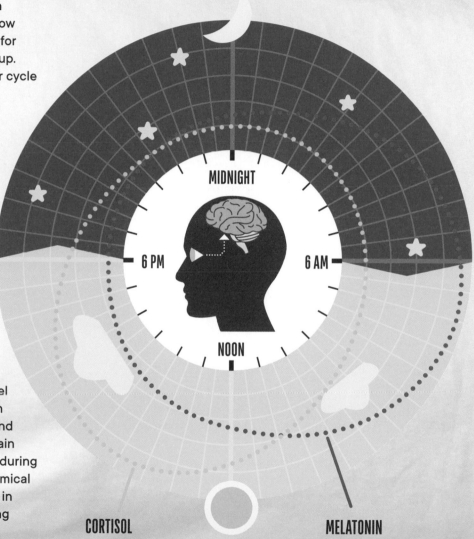

MIDNIGHT

6 PM

6 AM

NOON

CORTISOL

MELATONIN

WHY DO WE YAWN?

Birds, fish, reptiles and mammals are all known to yawn, but why do we do it? Scientists think there are a number of possible reasons...

* **Sleepiness** Yawns often happen when we're feeling drowsy and are one way our body tries to stay awake.
* **Boredom** If we're not feeling stimulated, we can feel sleepy.
* **Brain protection** It's thought yawning might help keep our brain at the right temperature and prevent it from overheating – if you're feeling hot-headed, try yawning!

HOW MUCH SLEEP DO WE NEED?

The amount of sleep we need depends on our age. Babies need a lot of shut-eye (around 16 hours a day), while teenagers need around 9 hours. As people get older they sleep for shorter periods of time.

Stage	Age	Sleep
NEWBORN	0-3 MONTHS	14-17 HOURS
INFANT	4-11 MONTHS	12-15 HOURS
TODDLER	1-2 YEARS	11-14 HOURS
PRESCHOOL	3-5 YEARS	10-13 HOURS
SCHOOL-AGE	6-13 YEARS	9-11 HOURS
TEEN	14-17 YEARS	8-10 HOURS
YOUNG ADULT	18-25 YEARS	7-9 HOURS
ADULT	26-64 YEARS	7-9 HOURS
OLDER	65+ YEARS	7-8 HOURS

Sleep cycles

Once we've fallen asleep we follow a sleep cycle that has four stages that repeat through the night until we wake up.

* In stage one of the cycle, our muscles relax and our brain waves, heartbeat, breathing and eye movements start to slow down.
* Stage two sees us falling into a deeper sleep and becoming even more relaxed.
* In stage three, we're the most relaxed we'll get, with our heart rate, breathing and brain activity all reaching their lowest levels.
* The fourth stage is known as rapid eye movement (REM) sleep. Our first REM sleep happens about 90 minutes after we nod off. During this stage, our eyes move back and forth quickly under our eyelids. This stage is when we usually have dreams! It's thought this REM sleep is linked to converting recent experiences into memories.

Sleepwalking

Sleepwalking (also called somnambulism) is when someone gets out of bed and walks about – all while they're still asleep! One in five people sleepwalk at least once in their life, and it usually happens during deep sleep. It's not known why people sleepwalk, but it's thought to run in families and is more likely to happen if someone's not getting enough shut-eye.

Sleep talking

Sleep talking (also known as somniloquy) is when someone mumbles or starts talking when they're asleep. It's not known why people do it, but it's thought we all talk in our sleep at least once!

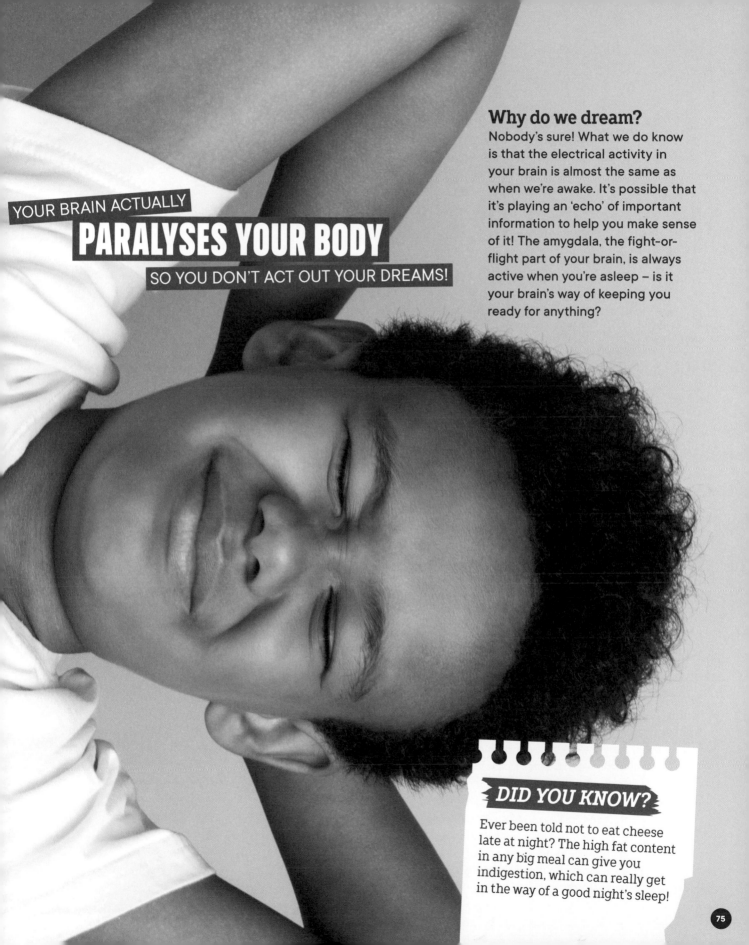

YOUR BRAIN ACTUALLY

PARALYSES YOUR BODY

SO YOU DON'T ACT OUT YOUR DREAMS!

Why do we dream?

Nobody's sure! What we do know is that the electrical activity in your brain is almost the same as when we're awake. It's possible that it's playing an 'echo' of important information to help you make sense of it! The amygdala, the fight-or-flight part of your brain, is always active when you're asleep – is it your brain's way of keeping you ready for anything?

DID YOU KNOW?

Ever been told not to eat cheese late at night? The high fat content in any big meal can give you indigestion, which can really get in the way of a good night's sleep!

GERM ALERT!

If you had super-vision, you'd be able to spot tons of strange-looking critters crawling over your body at this very moment! What's more, loads of tiny life forms live inside your body too. Don't worry though, these micro-organisms are bacteria and viruses (also called germs) and while the idea of them might sound yucky, not all of them are bad. In fact, some of them actually help to keep you healthy...

What are germs?

Germs are microscopic organisms that are invisible to the naked eye. Sometimes harmful germs invade our bodies and can make us feel poorly by nabbing our body's nutrients and energy and releasing nasty toxins – chemicals that act like poisons. These toxins are the cause of annoying common infections, such as rashes and coughs.

The good news is that not all kinds of germs are bad for us. In fact, the human body is covered in millions of micro-organisms that don't do us any harm. Our skin, mouth and intestines are home to organisms that protect us from infection and keep our bodies working healthily. These friendly bacteria help us absorb nutrients from the food we eat, and turn the leftover bits into poo and pee to keep our stomachs working properly. They also help our body make vitamin K, so it can heal when it's injured and convert the carbohydrates we eat into energy!

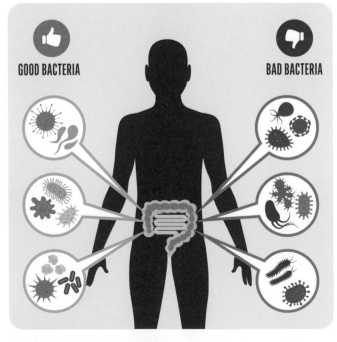

GOOD BACTERIA

BAD BACTERIA

▲ There are TRILLIONS of microorganisms living in your gut!

GERM ZONE

Meet the four main types of germs...

1 Bacteria

Tiny organisms that live on nutrients from their surroundings, like the body. Bacteria multiply as they cause infections, and can also reproduce outside of a host.

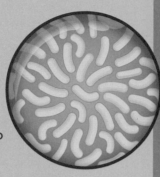

2 Viruses

Germs that need living cells to grow and reproduce. Viruses can't usually survive long if they're not inside a living thing. They cause flu, measles, chickenpox and lots of other illnesses in humans – including Covid-19.

3 Fungi

Plant-like organisms with lots of cells. Unlike other plants, fungi get nourishment from people, animals and plants. Lots of fungi aren't dangerous but they can cause some very uncomfortable infections, such as itchy rashes.

4 Protozoa

Single-celled germs that are most at home when they're in wet places and often spread diseases through water. In humans, some protozoa can cause sickness and diarrhoea.

Staying healthy

Most harmful germs are spread through the air – in sneezes, coughs and even breaths. Germs can also be spread by touching something contaminated. Imagine someone with a cold blowing their nose and then touching this book. The germs from their nose would end up on it and could transfer onto you the next time you picked it up!

So how do we stop germs from spreading, and protect ourselves from the harmful nasties that can make us ill? Check out these top tips...

☑ **Always wash your hands** Keep your mitts nice and clean by washing them after you've been outside, every time that you cough or sneeze, and after you've used the bathroom.

☑ **Stay strong** Having a healthy diet, exercising regularly and getting enough sleep will mean your body's better at beating the germs it comes into contact with.

☑ **Cover up** Cover your mouth with a tissue whenever you sneeze or cough, then throw it away. If you don't have a tissue, you can sneeze or cough into your elbow instead.

160KM/H

DID YOU KNOW?

Sneezes and coughs travel at 160km/h and can send around 100,000 contagious germs into the air!

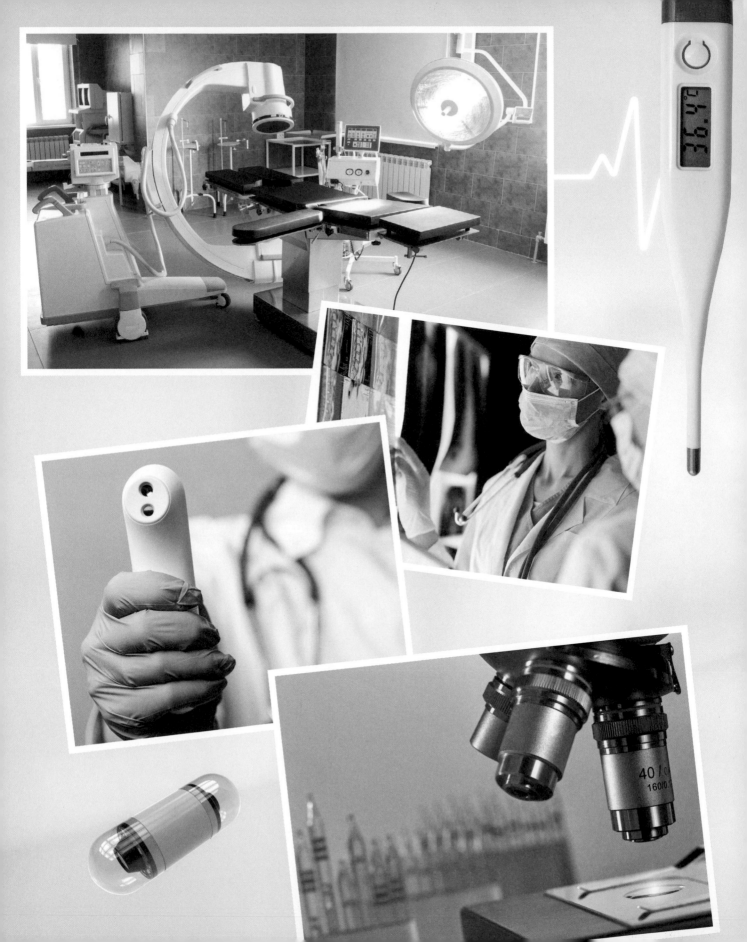

CHAPTER 3
MARVELLOUS MEDICINE

Even though our bodies are brilliant, sometimes things go wrong and we need medical science to put us right again. Read on to discover the miracles of modern medicine, from the equipment used to diagnose and treat illnesses to the work being done to eradicate nasty tropical diseases...

THE HISTORY OF
MEDICINE

Humans have searched for ways to cure illness and injuries for thousands of years. These milestones changed the history of medicine forever

HOLEY HEALING

Brain surgery is one of the most complex procedures a patient can undergo, but historians have found proof that as far back as 7,000 years ago, early humans were trying out trepanning – it's a painful process that involves making holes in the skull to relieve everything from abscesses to blindness. Ancient skulls found in Peru proved that some people even survived!

CRAZIEST CURE Digging into the skull might seem extreme, but ancient physicians believed it released evil forces from the patient.

MAGIC AND MEDICINE

Nearly 5,000 years ago in 2,650BC, records show that the ancient Egyptian healer Imhotep created treatments for hundreds of diseases. Ancient doctors across the world mixed magic spells with herbal cures and creams. Imhotep's effect on medicine was so legendary that he was later worshipped by the Egyptians, as well as the ancient Greeks and Romans.

CRAZIEST CURE Egyptians had specialised doctors, but lots of their treatments were disgusting, and they didn't work. A papyrus guide from 1,500BC recommended using dog and donkey poo to ward off bad spirits – and probably anyone else!

THE BODY'S BALANCE

In 2,500BC, great thinkers in ancient China thought that the body was tied to the universe in a perfect balance of Yin and Yang. Early doctors' diagnoses came from the patient's dreams, smells and tastes – thousands of herbal remedies harnessed the power of plants, and acupuncture was often used for pain relief.

CRAZIEST CURE Mercury is famously toxic, but doctors have been using it as medicine for millennia. Chinese emperor Qin Shi Huang died because doctors told him eating it would make him immortal!

REWRITING THE RULES

In 500BC, the Indian physician Sushruta wrote a huge list of early medical tools and cures and became a pioneer of surgery. Eighty years later, a great thinker from ancient Greece called Hippocrates said that diseases were natural and not magical. He wrote the Hippocratic Oath, a code of conduct doctors still follow today, and recommended everything from better diets to plenty of exercise.

CRAZIEST CURE The Greeks gave us a good understanding of medicine, but Hippocrates thought the body was split into four 'humours' – black bile, yellow bile, phlegm and blood. He balanced these by draining blood and making patients throw up!

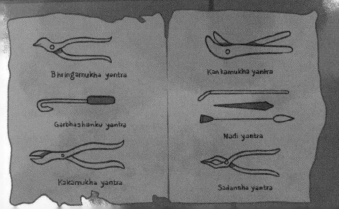

Bhringamukha yantra

Kan kamukha yantra

Garbhashanku yantra

Nadi yantra

Kakamukha yantra

Sadansha yantra

BLOOD

YELLOW BILE

BLACK BILE

PHLEGM

HOW HUMANS WORK

For centuries after Hippocrates, scientists started to learn more hidden truths about the human body. It was forbidden to dissect (cut up) humans in ancient Rome, so the Greek doctor Galen used apes and pigs as his subjects in the 2nd century AD. Romans saw how important cleanliness was to good health and surgeons learned to sterilise their tools with boiling water.

CRAZIEST CURE The ancient Romans might have pioneered plenty of life-saving techniques, but Pliny the Elder believed that dried camel brains could cure epilepsy, and eating mice would get rid of toothache.

GALENVS

THE CHURCH'S CURE

In the following centuries, churches set up the first hospitals and cared for the sick. Medical schools were built, starting with Italy's Schola Medica Salernitana in the 9th century. The ideas of Hippocrates and Galen spread across the world, and in 1242, Ibn al-Nafis discovered the truth about blood beating between the heart and lungs. A major medical revolution was just beginning!

CRAZIEST CURE Scientists believed that the stars in the night's sky influenced everything down here on Earth from birth to blood. By the end of the 15th century, Europe's physicians had to check the position of the moon before performing surgery!

MAKING THE CUT

By the 16th century, physicians had begun to think about the body in greater detail. In 1543, Andreas Vesalius published a book based on human anatomy and dissection and in 1628, William Harvey explained that the heart pumped blood around the body. Better book printing technology spread these exciting ideas around the world, and word started to spread about this new science.

CRAZIEST CURE Vesalius persuaded a judge to pass a new law that let him dissect dead criminals – yikes! This breakthrough helped him prove that lots of Galen's ancient theories were actually false.

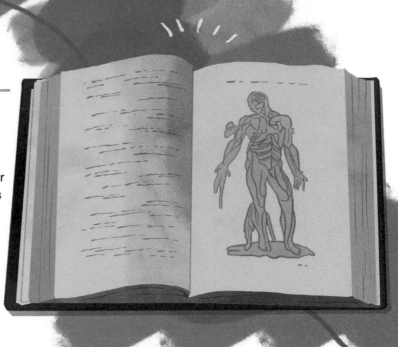

NEARLY MODERN MEDICINE

As schools of science uncovered more about the natural world, physicians worked hard to find cures for diseases and illnesses that had been recorded for thousands of years. In 1665, Robert Hooke used a microscope to study specimens and identified the first 'cell'. In 1796, Edward Jenner experimented with the body's natural defences and discovered vaccination and immunology. Injecting a tiny amount of pus into a patient, he proved that the body could develop its own defences for fighting off diseases – we still use this method today!

CRAZIEST CURE Physicians had to be really fast! Before numbing anaesthetics stopped pain from spreading, Robert Liston became famous for amputating legs in just 30 seconds flat. Ouch!

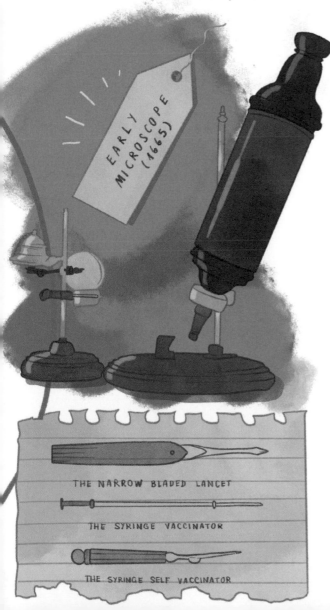

EARLY MICROSCOPE (1665)

THE NARROW BLADED LANCET

THE SYRINGE VACCINATOR

THE SYRINGE SELF VACCINATOR

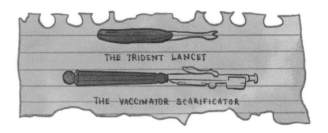

THE TRIDENT LANCET

THE VACCINATOR SCARIFICATOR

LIFE-SAVING MACHINES

Whether doctors are listening to your heartbeat, keeping track of the tiny bacteria on your skin or looking inside your body, amazing inventions play a huge part in keeping us all healthy. Check out some of the world's most awesome medical equipment...

DID YOU KNOW?

No, the 'X' in 'X-ray' doesn't stand for 'extraordinary'! It stands for 'unknown' because the radiation X-rays use was unknown when they were invented. They're also known as radiography.

X-RAY MACHINE

Discovered by German physicist Wilhelm Röntgen in 1895, X-rays are a form of radiation – waves of energy that are much more powerful than regular light. These super-powerful light waves are really useful because they can show us pictures of what the inside of an object – such as a body, or even a suitcase – looks like. This means doctors and dentists can use X-rays to see internal signs of damage or injury with their patients. That's cool, right?

X-rays are awesomely powerful! Not only are they vital in biology, but they are still used in space agencies' most powerful telescopes.

THERMOMETER

Thermometers are used to measure the temperature of things (how hot or cold they are). Scientists have used this clever bit of kit for hundreds of years, with the first one – which was called a thermoscope – created by Italian inventor Galileo Galilei in 1593. Since the earliest days of medical history, doctors have recognised that the human body gets hotter when we're feeling under the weather, so thermometers are very useful!

3 FAST FACTS

(1) A thermometer invented by Thomas Allbutt in 1867 took five minutes to take someone's temperature.

(2) Thermometers developed after World War II used infrared technology, and were placed in the ear.

(3) Modern thermometers use electrical sensors to measure our temperature.

ELECTRON MICROSCOPE

Microscopes are devices that make tiny objects look larger. Optical microscopes (also called light microscopes) work like magnifying glasses, using curved pieces of glass or plastic to bend light and make objects that are too small to see with our eyes look bigger.

If scientists want to get an even closer look at tiny objects, they use electron microscopes. These instruments magnify objects by using beams of electrons – very small pieces of matter and energy – instead of light. This amazing magnifying power can help scientists understand how diseases work.

3 FAST FACTS

(1) Electron microscopes can magnify objects up to two million times!

(2) The first electron microscope was invented in 1933 by German electrical engineer Ernst Ruska.

(3) Objects can only be seen with an electron microscope if they're in an airless space (a vacuum), so they can't be used to study living things.

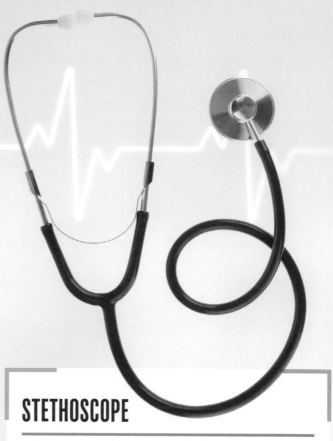

DEFIBRILLATOR

Discovered by Jean-Louis Prévost and Frédéric Batelli in 1899, a defibrillator is a device that's used to help people having problems with their heart. Defibrillators work by giving a controlled electric shock straight to the heart, which helps restore a normal heartbeat. The defibrillator's high energy shock can be used to help hearts that are beating too slow or too fast or have suddenly stopped beating altogether.

HOW AMAZING?!

In 1965 a heart doctor from Northern Ireland called Frank Pantridge invented a portable defibrillator that could be powered by a car battery!

STETHOSCOPE

Stethoscopes are used by doctors and medical people to assess how their patient's body is working. The stethoscope is placed near the patient's heart or on their back to measure their heartbeat or breathing. Stethoscopes can even be used to listen to the sound of someone's veins to make sure their blood is flowing around their body properly!

Invented in 1816 by French doctor René Laënnec, the stethoscope started out as a wooden tube and could only be used with one ear. However, stethoscopes have developed over the last two hundred years and are now Y-shaped and used with both ears!

BUT HOW DOES IT WORK?

The stethoscope doctors use today works a lot like your eardrum. The flat diaphragm picks up on your body's vibrations, and the tube funnels them straight to the ear.

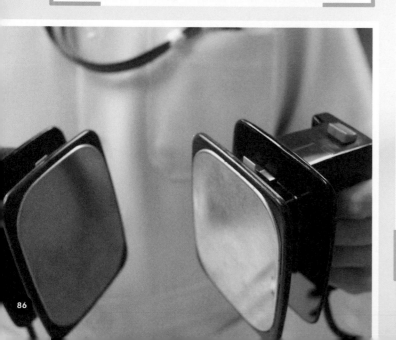

ENDOSCOPE

Technology has changed the way we see inside the body. Endoscope tech is over 200 years old, and it allows specialists to use flexible, thin tubes with a powerful light and camera at one end to observe images inside the body and project them onto a screen.

These thin tubes are versatile and can be inserted down the throat or up the bottom. Endoscopes with tiny tools at the end can even be used for surgery, and they're also vital for technicians taking samples. This is called biopsy and it can be lifesaving when it's used to diagnose problems. Investigating internal issues like this isn't usually painful for the patient and it can be done while they're awake, making things much safer and easier.

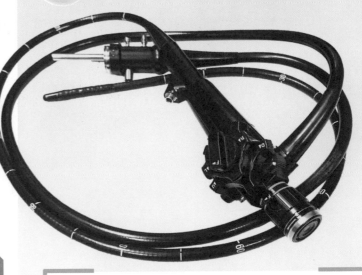

New digital endoscope technology is pill-sized! It's **wireless, swallowable** and designed to pass through the entire digestive system!

BUT HOW DOES IT WORK?

Light bounces down bunches of glass fibres and illuminates the end of the endoscope. The image then travels back up the tube and is displayed on a screen.

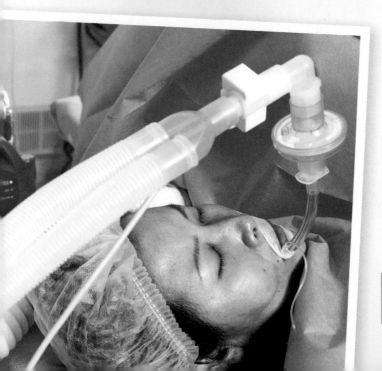

VENTILATORS

To help you to breathe, muscles in your ribcage move to draw air into the lungs and then relax so that you exhale. When someone's respiratory system isn't working as it should, mechanical ventilators do this work for them.

A ventilator provides the patient with a steady source of air via either a face mask or a tube that goes down the windpipe. It uses pressure to copy the normal rhythm of the lungs and keeps the airflow at a comfortable temperate, adding just the right amount of moisture, so it doesn't shock the system!

BUT HOW DOES IT WORK?

Ventilators use pressure to copy the body's breathing and supply the millions of tiny balloons in your lungs called alveoli with an oxygen-rich supply of air.

TROPICAL TERRORS!

Bursting blood cells, non-stop toilet visits and squirming skin... These are real symptoms of illnesses known as tropical diseases. Read on to find out more about these awful ailments – and how they're cured!

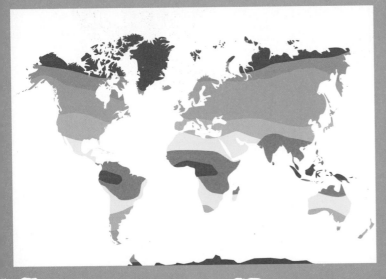

Around a third of the planet's population live in the tropics – areas found on or near the equator (an imaginary line around the middle of the planet) halfway between the North and South Poles. Because of where they are, these places have tropical climates and get more sunshine than anywhere else on the planet. The tropics are often home to beautiful sandy beaches, picture-perfect palm trees and lush tropical rainforests. However, these sunny places are also home to tropical diseases – infectious illnesses that thrive in hot, humid conditions...

 Tropical zone

Weather issues

Tropical climates are usually warm and wet, thanks to year-round high temperatures and lots of rain. Their air holds lots of moisture, which is great news for the exotic plants and crops that grow there – they love this kind of weather – but it also attracts insects, which can cause problems as they are responsible for some tropical diseases spreading.

Blast from the past

Research has shown tropical diseases have been around since ancient times. Famous ancient Greek and Roman doctors wrote about them, and scientists have uncovered evidence that suggests tropical diseases were even around in ancient Egypt!

Thought of as the father of medicine, Greek doctor Hippocrates wrote about tropical diseases way back in 400BC – a whopping 2,400 years ago!

FEARSOME FIVE

Check out these five tropical nasties!

2 CHOLERA

People pick up cholera from drinking water or eating food that's contaminated with a bacteria called Vibrio cholerae. The bacteria releases a poison that makes the body jettison large amounts of water – leading to non-stop diarrhoea, tummy ache and sickness. Luckily, if it's caught early, cholera is easy to treat. Taking antibiotics and replacing the lost fluids will normally cure the illness in a week.

1 MALARIA

This tropical disease is spread by mosquitoes that are infected by a parasite. The mosquitoes pass on the illness when they bite people. The parasite invades the person's bloodstream and multiplies until the infected blood cells burst and release more of the blood-bashing parasites into their host!

Malaria causes chills, fever, headaches and nausea, but medication usually cures it in a couple of weeks. However, people who live in areas where malaria is common are often reinfected and don't get to recover between their infections.

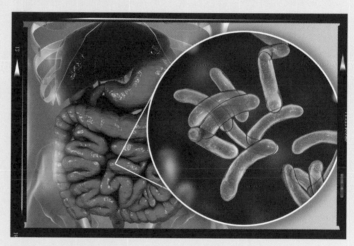

Malaria is one of the world's oldest diseases, and sadly claims almost half a million lives each year. The good news is that sleeping under insecticide-treated mosquito nets protects people while they sleep. Plus, scientists have discovered a microbe that prevents mosquitoes from being able to spread malaria parasites – so it could soon be a thing of the past!

3 LEPROSY

This tropical disease has been around since ancient times and affects the skin and nerves. Leprosy (also known as Hansen's disease) is caused by a bacteria, and is spread from person to person by coughing and sneezing, which transfers yucky infected droplets. Luckily leprosy isn't very contagious, and is curable with antibiotics.

TODAY, 95% OF PEOPLE ARE ACTUALLY
IMMUNE TO LEPROSY

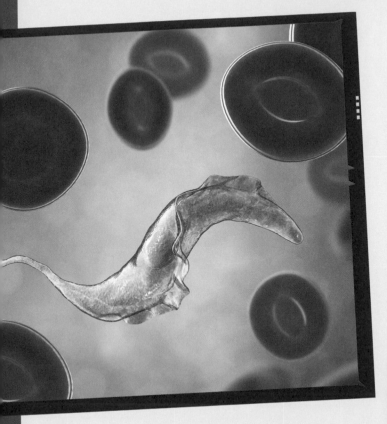

5 BOTFLIES

These insects have a pretty sneaky way of spreading disease! Botflies latch onto a mosquito mid-flight and attach their eggs to its stomach. Then, once the mosquito bites someone, the eggs hatch and burrow into the wound left by the bite!

After a month or so, the botfly eggs turn into larvae and dig their way out from under the skin – so they can drop to the ground, grow into flies and repeat the gross cycle! People infected with botflies have sore, itchy wounds and can feel the larva squirming under their skin. Botfly infestation is treated by tweezing the flies from the wound. These guys really get under the skin!

4 SLEEPING SICKNESS

Infected tsetse flies spread this nasty disease by nibbling on people, which transfers parasites, called Trypanosoma brucei. Sleeping sickness has two stages – fever, headaches, itching and joint pain are first. Then the second stage sees the parasite infecting the host's nervous system, disturbing their sleep and affecting their brain! Untreated, sleeping sickness is fatal, but can be cured if it's spotted early.

DID YOU KNOW?

Scientists are currently studying how genetically modifying mosquitoes could cure illnesses and how it might affect the planet in the future.

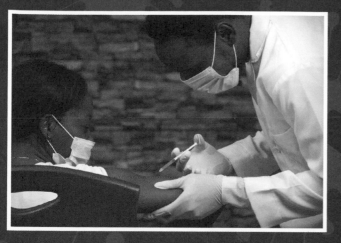

WHAT IS A VACCINE?

A vaccine is a type of medicine that stops us from getting an illness. Vaccines work by showing our body how to recognise and fight off viruses and bacteria. This is done by introducing a special version of the germ into your body. It can't make you ill because the germ in the vaccine has either been weakened, killed, or is only part of itself.

The vaccine works like a practice run and gives your body an idea of what harmful germs it might need to deal with in the future. Once your body's fought off the germ, it remembers how to beat it. So if the germ enters your body again, your system will automatically get rid of it before you become ill, or at least lessen the effects!

When lots of people are vaccinated and protected from an infection, it's harder for it to spread in a community. This effect is called 'herd immunity'.

▲ In this diagram, if the infected red person comes into contact with the vaccinated blue people, the virus is less likely to spread to the unvaccinated green people.

THE BIG
BODY QUIZ

Read the book, then put your newfound knowledge to the test!

1. Roughly how many cells are there in the human body? (*Turn to p6 for a hint*)

2. What system pumps the blood around your body? (*Turn to p9 for a hint*)

3. What is the name for the thin top layer of skin? (*Turn to p11 for a hint*)

4. What are skin, hair and nails made from? (*Turn to p15 for a hint*)

5. Where is the stapes bone found? (*Turn to p17 for a hint*)

6. How much blood does the heart pump daily? (*Turn to p21 for a hint*)

7. What is the length of all the neurons in your body lined up together? (*Turn to p27 for a hint*)

8. What did the ancient Egyptians believe was the centre of the body? (*Turn to p31 for a hint*)

9. What protects your lungs? (*Turn to p33 for a hint*)

10. Where is poo stored when it's ready to be ejected from the human body? (*Turn to p35 for a hint*)

11. What percentage of our DNA do we share with chimpanzees? (*Turn to p38 for a hint*)

12. How many chromosomes does a zygote have? (*Turn to p41 for a hint*)

13. What gland in your brain starts to release hormones at the onset of puberty? (*Turn to p45 for a hint*)

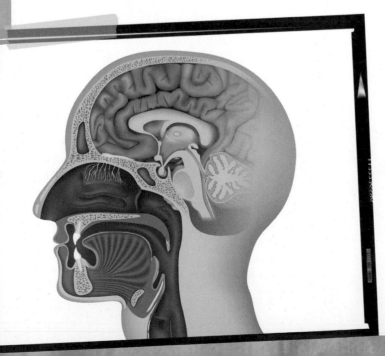

14 What type of white blood cell chews up invading germs? (*Turn to p48 for a hint*)

15 What is the scientific name for a rumbling tummy? (*Turn to p52 for a hint*)

16 What is the jelly-like substance that fills most of your eye? (*Turn to p54 for a hint*)

17 What is the last space where smell chemicals are processed before being sent to the brain? (*Turn to p58 for a hint*)

18 How many types of papillae are there in your mouth? (*Turn to p62 for a hint*)

19 What do Merkel's discs react to? (*Turn to p66 for a hint*)

20 What is the loudness of a sound measured in? (*Turn to p70 for a hint*)

21 How long does the average person dream? (*Turn to p73 for a hint*)

22 How fast do sneezes and coughs travel? (*Turn to p77 for a hint*)

23 How quickly could the skilled physician Robert Liston amputate legs? (*Turn to p83 for a hint*)

24 In what year was the electron microscope first invented? (*Turn to p85 for a hint*)

25 Who wrote about tropical diseases in 400BC? (*Turn to p88 for a hint*)

GLOSSARY

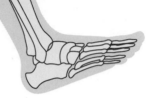

ABSCESSES
Painful collections of pus in parts of the body.

ATOM
A microscopic particle of matter, made from protons and neutrons surrounded by a cloud of electrons.

CALCIUM
A metallic chemical element.

CELL
The tiny parts that make up and structure everything in the human body.

CHYME
A fluid made of partly digested food and gastric juices from the stomach.

COLLAGEN
A protein that structures various tissues in the body, like the skin.

CONTAGIOUS
A disease or condition that can be spread from one living thing to another.

DIAGNOSES
When illnesses or other conditions affecting a patient are identified by examination of the symptoms.

EMBRYO
The earliest stage of an unborn living thing, after fertilisation has happened.

EVOLUTION
The process by which living things have changed and developed into different species over many millions of years.

FERTILISED
When a new living thing is created when a male sperm combines with a female egg in the womb.

HORMONES
Substances produced in the body that stimulate specific cells, tissues and processes, like growing.

HYDRATED
When something has absorbed enough water.

LOBE
A roundish part of an organ, like the parts of the brain.

LUBRICATE
When something is made wet and slippery so that it can be moved more easily and with less friction.

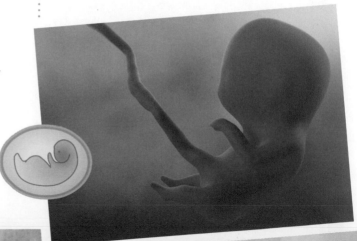

MAMMALIAN
Relating to mammals, a group of warm-blooded vertebrate animals that have hair or fur and give birth to live young.

METABOLISM
All the chemical reactions that happen inside a living thing in order to keep it alive.

MOLECULE
A group of atoms joined together.

NUTRIENTS
The substances in food that are needed to keep the body of a person or other living thing alive and healthy.

PIGMENT
The material in living things like animals or plants that gives them their colour.

PRIMATE
An order of species of mammals, including monkeys, apes and humans.

RADIATION
Energy or particles that come from something and travel across space, often in waves.

SALIVA
A watery liquid produced in the mouth that helps you to chew up and swallow food.

SINUSES
An empty space in the bones of the face behind the nose.

SYSTEM
A group of things that work together.

TISSUE
The different types of collections of cells of which a living organism, like a human, is made.

TOXIC
When something is poisonous or harmful to a living organism.

QUIZ ANSWERS

1. 30 trillion
2. Circulatory system
3. Epidermis
4. Keratin
5. The middle ear
6. 9,000 litres
7. 956km
8. The heart
9. The rib cage
10. The rectum
11. Nearly 99%
12. 46
13. Pituitary
14. Phagocytes
15. Borborygmus
16. Vitreous fluid
17. Olfactory bulb
18. Four
19. Light pressure
20. Decibels
21. Two hours a night
22. 160km/h
23. 30 seconds
24. 1933
25. Hippocrates

INDEX

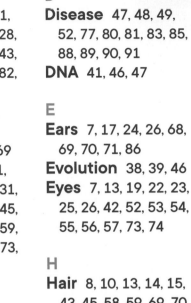

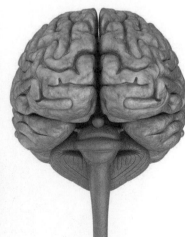

First published 2023 by Button Books, an imprint of Guild of Master Craftsman Publications Ltd, Castle Place, 166 High Street, Lewes, East Sussex, BN7 1XU, UK. Copyright in the Work © GMC Publications Ltd, 2023. ISBN 978 1 78708 134 5. Distributed by Publishers Group West in the United States. All rights reserved. No part of this publication may be reproduced, stored in a retrieval system, or transmitted in any form or by any means without the prior permission of the publisher and copyright owner. While every effort has been made to obtain permission from the copyright holders for all material used in this book, the publishers will be pleased to hear from anyone who has not been appropriately acknowledged and to make the correction in future reprints. The publishers and authors can accept no legal responsibility for any consequences arising from the application of information, advice, or instructions given in this publication.
A catalogue record for this book is available from the British Library. Editorial: Susie Duff, Nick Pierce, Lauren Jarvis, Sam Taylor, Vincent Vincent. Design: Jo Chapman, Tim Lambert. Publisher: Jonathan Grogan. Production: Jim Bulley. Photos/illustrations: Shutterstock.com, illustrations: Michelle Urra. Colour origination by GMC Reprographics. Printed and bound in China.